D1415195

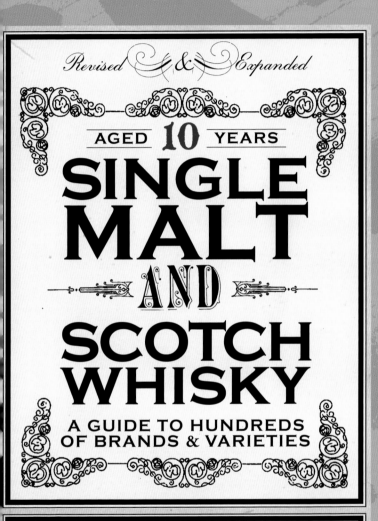

Revised & Expanded

AGED **10** YEARS

SINGLE MALT AND SCOTCH WHISKY

A GUIDE TO HUNDREDS OF BRANDS & VARIETIES

Daniel Lerner | *Hundreds of Varieties*

DISTILLED AND AGED BY BLACK DOG & LEVENTHAL PUBLISHERS

BLACK DOG & LEVENTHAL PUBLISHERS

Published by
Black Dog & Leventhal Publishers, Inc.
151 West 19th Street
New York, NY 10011

Printed in China

Interior and cover design: Ohioboy Design / Andy Taray

Photo research: Sarah Parvis

ISBN-13: 978-1-57912-577-6

h g f e

Library of Congress Cataloging-in-Publication data is on file at
Black Dog & Leventhal Publishers, Inc.

CONTENTS

INTRODUCTION

1. THE VIEW FROM BEN NEVIS, THE HIGHEST POINT IN SCOTLAND.
2. A QUAINT BRIDGE OVER THE RIVER DEE.
3. HEATHER-COVERED HILLS DOT THE LANDSCAPE OF SCOTLAND.

Imagine the Scottish Highlands around AD 500. A savagely beautiful landscape—rolling heather and peat-covered hills, pure water flowing from burns and springs, fields of ripe, golden barley gently swaying in the summer Highland breeze. The procedure for producing a fermented, low-alcohol beverage was already known by this time, and Highlanders were already enjoying a primitive form of beer.

The production of alcoholic beverages is considered a significant marker of civilization. The Chinese and ancient Greeks, for example, both produced crudely distilled alcoholic drinks. There is evidence of the distillation process in Britain long before the arrival of the Romans. However, that too was still rudimentary. Unlike the beer of our day, the stuff that Highlanders drank more than 1,500 years ago must have resembled thin, alcoholic oatmeal.

When the Moors arrived in Europe some time between the ninth and tenth centuries, they brought with them a sophisticated process of distillation originally developed to make fragrances, which was adapted to make spirits from fermented grains. In Britain in the early part of the sixteenth century, because of the

DEWAR'S WAS ONE OF THE FIRST BLENDED WHISKIES; THIS BOTTLE IS FROM THE 1880S.

perception that whisky possessed medicinal and curative powers, the Guild of Surgeon Barbers was given a monopoly on the production of whisky.

The first distillery officially documented was erected sometime in the 1670s, although distillation was occurring well before this time. Ironically, the whisky made by the unlicensed distilleries was said to be of a higher quality than the product made by the "official" distilleries because smugglers did not have to follow the draconian governmental guidelines regulating alcoholic strength and other levels of concentration. By the early nineteenth century, many illicit distilleries became licensed. Many more new distilleries were built on the sites of former illicit stills. Often the smugglers themselves were recruited to run these new legitimate operations, because of their prior experience.

Andrew Usher, who was an agent for Glenlivet Distillery, famous even in 1853, came up with the first vatted malt and gave it a proprietary name, Usher's Old Vatted Glenlivet. A specified blend of malt whiskies of various designated ages, Usher's recipe could be predictably reproduced. Up until this point, blending was used to hide the flaws of cheaper whisky by adding small amounts of good malt. Whisky was delivered to wholesalers in either wooden casks or stone jars. Then the blending was done by grocers, wine and spirit merchants, and inn owners. But with Usher's Old Vatted

THE MASTER BLENDER INSPECTS A NEW BOWMORE SPIRIT.

Glenlivet, an affordable good drink was now available in a bottle and made available to the general public. Other blended recipes developed during this period, including Dewar's, Haig, and Johnnie Walker. Between the new ease of production and transportation and a high-quality product, whisky exporting flourished.

Starting in 1860 and lasting until the late 1890s, a vine-killing microscopic bug called *phylloxera* destroyed most of the vineyards in France. Because no grapes were available, brandy could no longer be produced in commercial quantities. Scotch filled the gap in that market and fully established itself as a desirable and sought-after beverage all over the world.

Since 1900, the popularity of malt whisky has gone through several cycles of expansion and contraction. The major events of the twentieth century—World War I, the Great Depression, Prohibition, and World War II—severely impacted the production and consumption of whisky. After each of these catastrophic events, however, the whisky industry revived itself. Through intense determination, perseverance, and skill, whisky makers continue to produce to this day a great variety of whiskies of consistently high quality, great breed, and distinct style. Times have never been better for lovers of malt.

CHAPTER **1** CHAPTER

HOW TO USE
THIS BOOK

The goal in writing this guide is to provide easily accessible information about the history, production methods, current trends, availability, and tasting profiles of single malt and Scotch whisky.

At first blush, the world of whisky can seem a bit daunting in its variety and complexity. There are many different distilleries, around one hundred by last count, many of which produce and bottle a profusion of whiskies. Add to this the explosive growth of the independent bottling movement. The independent bottlers provide us with whiskies from individual casks, usually at cask strength, single-vintage bottlings, and library ranges, which include numerous vintages from a single distillery. Wood-finished whiskies—that is, whiskies that spend some additional aging time in barrels made from various kinds of woods—have recently become popularized. Just to further complicate the issue, all of these ranges are available in both official distillery bottlings and independent bottlings. New vatted malts, single-grain whiskies, and a continually expanding catalog of blended whiskies continue to enter the market. It's no wonder the consumer is overwhelmed.

This guide explores the world of whisky one step at a time. First, the history of whisky is discussed, outlining the development of the distilleries and the refinement of the distillation process. This is followed by an explanation of production methods. The malt whisky regions are described, and examples of various whiskies are cited that illustrate each region's individual and unique characteristics. "What's on the Label" provides definitions of bottling, labeling, and aging terms. There is a discussion of aging and bottling regimens, as well as statistical information relating to the whisky industry and the worldwide market. One indispensable section is the alphabetical guide giving the individual single malts with descriptions, tasting notes, and distillery contact information. A listing of currently available blended whiskies with tasting notes follows. A glossary of terms and a resource guide for further exploration conclude the guide.

IN 2004, 88.4 MILLION CASES OF SCOTCH WHISKY WERE SOLD IN OVER TWO HUNDRED MARKETS WORLDWIDE. THAT EQUALS THIRTY BOTTLES EVERY SECOND.

CHAPTER **2** CHAPTER

THE DISTILLING PROCESS:

NO ORDINARY TRICKLE

PEAT IS USED TO FUEL THE FIRE THAT DRIES THE MALTED BARLEY.

The word *distill* derives from the Latin *destillare,* "to trickle or drip down." Alcohol boils, conveniently, at a lower temperature than water. This simple rule is the basis for all distilling. Hot, boiled vapors are directed into tubes cooled by immersion in water. The result is condensation, in which the cooling vapors trickle back into a liquid state. But this description oversimplifies a time-honored, laborious process and the sublime product it yields. Making Scotch whisky is more like this:

1. Pick some ripe barley.

2. Submerge it in local spring water for several days.

3. Spread out the soaked grain on a large flat surface—the floor of a barn will do nicely—and, during the course of the next eight to ten days, turn it over each day with a large, flat, wooden shovel. Why? Because it helps the barley to begin to germinate—to begin to sprout. Inside each grain, enzymes are converting starch to sugar. More later on how these sugars are converted to alcohol.

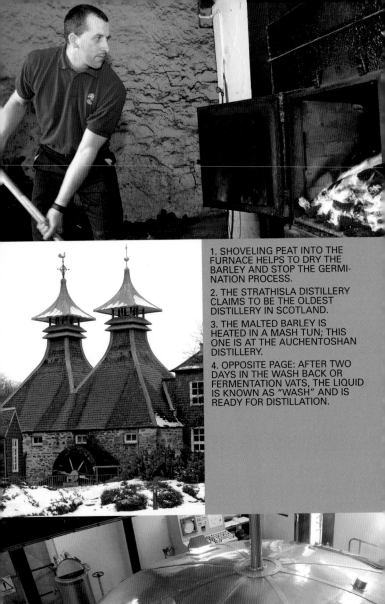

1. SHOVELING PEAT INTO THE FURNACE HELPS TO DRY THE BARLEY AND STOP THE GERMINATION PROCESS.

2. THE STRATHISLA DISTILLERY CLAIMS TO BE THE OLDEST DISTILLERY IN SCOTLAND.

3. THE MALTED BARLEY IS HEATED IN A MASH TUN; THIS ONE IS AT THE AUCHENTOSHAN DISTILLERY.

4. OPPOSITE PAGE: AFTER TWO DAYS IN THE WASH BACK OR FERMENTATION VATS, THE LIQUID IS KNOWN AS "WASH" AND IS READY FOR DISTILLATION.

4. Take this wet, barely germinated barley and spread it out on the floor of a large kiln to malt. (When you visit a distillery in Scotland, look for the malting shed. It is the low building with the interesting pagoda-shaped ventilator on the roof.) Start a fire under the floor, fueling it with peat; it works well and there is a lot of it close by. This step stops the barley from further germinating and—a nice bonus—peat, which is composed of highly compressed organic material, smokes when it burns. This smoke impregnates the grain and leaves a lovely smoky, peaty flavor in the finished product.

5. Clean the grain and grind it by passing it through a grist mill.

6. Place the grist in a large vat and add hot water. The local water often has trace minerals and some "peaty" quality, which imparts additional flavoring elements. The remaining starch in the grist is converted into sugar, which is then dissolved into solution. Repeat this cycle of draining and adding hot water several times. You have now produced *wort,* a sweet liquid.

7. Drain the liquid into a large, deep wooden or stainless-steel vat and add brewer's and/or distiller's yeast. (Use the leftover stuff, i.e., husks and depleted grain, for high-quality cattle feed.) There's lots of action for the next two or three days: boiling, steaming, and frothing. Fermentation is happening. (If you are a citizen of AD 500, you know how to do all this because, so far, the process pretty much resembles the way you make beer.)

8. Now you are ready to implement the new technology: fill a heavy cauldron with the fermented liquid, which contains 5 to 9 percent alcohol and is now called *wash.* Cover tightly. Place over a coal fire. Sticking out of the lid of the cauldron is a spout. Sprouting out of the spout is a coil of copper tubing. This coil is generally submerged in a barrel of cold water (or

1. THE DISTILLATION PROCESS, WHICH SEPARATES THE ALCOHOL FROM THE WASH, TAKES PLACE IN THESE HUGE COPPER POT STILLS.

2. THE DISTILLED SPIRIT IS POURED INTO THE OAK BARRELS THAT WILL BE USED FOR THE AGING PROCESS.

3. OPPOSITE PAGE: IN ORDER TO BE CONSIDERED SCOTCH WHISKY, THE LIQUID MUST SPEND AT LEAST THREE YEARS IN SCOTLAND IN CASKS IN AN AGING CELLAR.

some other arrangement, so long as cold water flows over the coils). As the vapors produced from the boiling of the wash rise through the spout and into the coils, the temperature changes inside. This causes the vapors, which contain oils, flavors, esters, alcohols, water, and various other pure and not so pure agents. These condense and drip down the coils, to be collected in some sort of receptacle. After you have run all the wash through your still and collected it, clean the still, refire it, and repeat the process.

9. Having completed this first distillation, you now have in your possession a quantity of liquid known as the *low wines* (which contain 20 to 25 percent alcohol). To purify and concentrate the flavors and alcohol of this liquid, you embark upon a second distillation. From experience, you know that at the beginning of this second distillation, the stuff that comes out first, called the *foreshots,* is still pretty impure and not very drinkable, so you drain it off and save it to distill again with the next batch. Now, finally the *middle cut,* the stuff you have worked so hard to produce, is drawn off. After this is completed, all the *feints,* that is, the remaining distillate, are drawn off and saved. This production is too impure and/or dilute to consume and will be mixed with the foreshots and the next batch of low wines for the next time you distill.

10. Mix a little gunpowder with a little of your whisky and light the mixture. If it doesn't light, it's not strong enough; if it explodes, it's too strong. If it burns steadily, you have *proof.*

11. Put the colorless whisky into casks. Sell most of your production to whisky merchants so you can pay the rent on the farm. These merchants will bottle it as they need it, selling right out of cask (no aging) for the average Joe and aged a bit in cask for the gentry. Of course, always keep a little for yourself to drink with your family and friends.

Whether it's 1494, the date of the first recorded purchase of malted barley for the production of Aqua Vitae; or 1690, when Ferintosh, the first distillery mentioned by name, suffered a fire; or 1932, when America's Prohibition was repealed; or 2004, when thirty bottles of Scotch whisky were sold overseas every minute—in five hundred years, the process of distilling malt whisky has remained fundamentally unchanged.

THE PROCESS

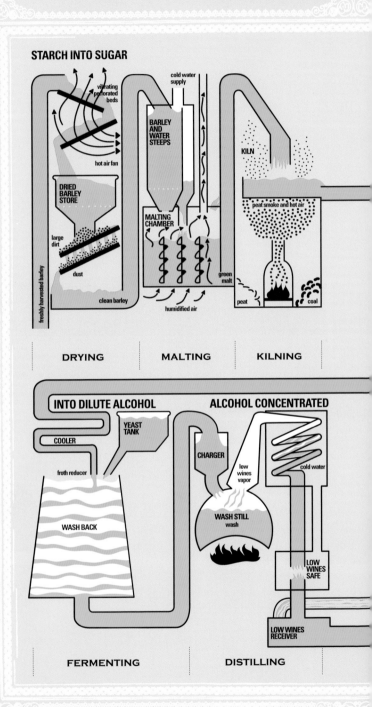

STARCH INTO SUGAR

vibrating perforated beds

hot air fan

cold water supply

BARLEY AND WATER STEEPS

KILN

DRIED BARLEY STORE

peat smoke and hot air

large dirt

MALTING CHAMBER

dust

green malt

freshly harvested barley

clean barley

humidified air

peat

coal

DRYING | **MALTING** | **KILNING**

INTO DILUTE ALCOHOL | **ALCOHOL CONCENTRATED**

COOLER

YEAST TANK

CHARGER

low wines vapor

cold water

froth reducer

WASH BACK

WASH STILL
wash

LOW WINES SAFE

LOW WINES RECEIVER

FERMENTING | **DISTILLING**

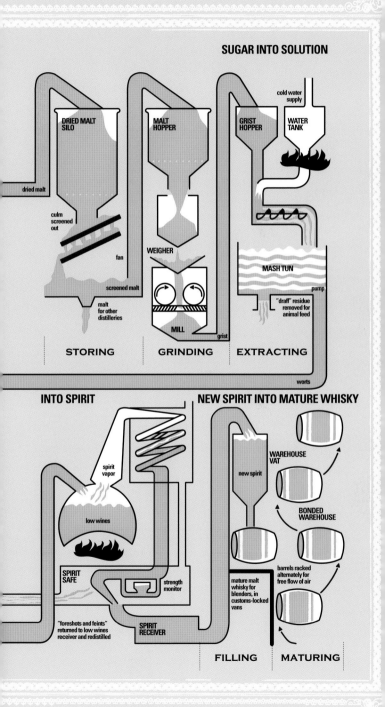

SUGAR INTO SOLUTION

cold water supply

DRIED MALT SILO

MALT HOPPER

GRIST HOPPER

WATER TANK

dried malt

culm screened out

fan

WEIGHER

screened malt

MASH TUN

pump

malt for other distilleries

"draff" residue removed for animal feed

MILL

grist

STORING   **GRINDING**   **EXTRACTING**

worts

INTO SPIRIT   NEW SPIRIT INTO MATURE WHISKY

spirit vapor

WAREHOUSE VAT

new spirit

low wines

BONDED WAREHOUSE

SPIRIT SAFE

strength monitor

barrels racked alternately for free flow of air

mature malt whisky for blenders, in customs-locked vans

"foreshots and feints" returned to low wines receiver and redistilled

SPIRIT RECEIVER

FILLING   **MATURING**

WHY SCOTCH WHISKY?

ISLANDS

SPEYSIDE

NORTHERN
HIGHLANDS

EASTERN
HIGHLANDS

CENTRAL
HIGHLANDS

WESTERN
HIGHLANDS

ISLAY

LOWLAND

CAMPBELTOWN

1. THE MALT WHISKY-
PRODUCING REGIONS
OF SCOTLAND.

2. PEAT CONTRIBUTES
TO THE DISTINCT
TASTE OF SCOTCH
WHISKY.

How did our ancestors discover the process and devise these methods of production? The distillation of whisky is fascinating, especially if one is inclined to contemplate its origins. As a testament to human ingenuity, its process is unrivaled in its efficiency and completeness. At the end of the day, however, we could be talking about distilling paint, ethanol, or rocket fuel, so easily is the basic principle replicated using other substances.

This being the case, we may now ask ourselves where, exactly, does Scotch whisky come from? From whence does this beautiful and poetic nectar, fully formed in each and every one of its individual manifestations, emerge? The immediate answer to that question is obviously Scotland, and, more specifically, several regions within that country as defined in the last century: the Highlands, the Lowlands, Islay, Campbeltown, and the Islands. The Highland region is further subdivided into North, South, East, West, and Speyside. The Islands encompass the islands of Skye, Mull, Jura, Arran, and Orkney.

Indeed, geography offers something of a clue to what makes this marvelous beverage marvelous. But there are other essentials:

- the amount and quality of peat used in the malting process

- the mineral content and flavor characteristics of the water used by the individual distillery

- the distillery's proximity to the ocean

- the type of barley

- the degree of its germination and the intensity of malting

- the style, shape, and general condition of the stills

- the experience of the still master, and last but not least,

- the kind of barrel used for aging and maturing of the distillate

Nor should we forget fairies, wood and water sprites, legendary historical figures, and a host of other mythological creatures that populate Scotland and its whisky industry.

NEW DEVELOPMENTS

Recent years have seen a great many changes in the production and marketing of single malt whisky. Much corporate jockeying has taken place. The result has been both a greater degree of concentration of distillery ownership in fewer corporate hands and, paradoxically, an increase in independent ownership. Close to 90 percent of all the distilleries in Scotland are owned by corporations, most of which are multinational. The remainder are either independently owned or are in partnership with independent bottlers.

Because no one can agree on the perfect aging regimen, or even the best kind of barrel to use in the production of making malt whisky, many distilleries now offer a range of whiskies. Contained within this range are whiskies of various ages and vintages, different alcoholic strengths, and different kinds of wood finishes. The notion of single-cask bottlings—whisky bottled at full strength (without dilution to bring down the proof) from a single cask—has taken hold.

Sophisticated whisky drinkers look for unique and unreproducible traits in their whisky. In addition, variations of more traditionally vatted whiskies are sought after, hence the wood-finished ranges, which are imbued with additional levels of flavor complexity by aging them in different types of wood.

THE TELFORD BRIDGE, CRAIGELLACHIE, CROSSES THE RIVER SPEY.

THE MALT WHISKY–PRODUCING REGIONS OF SCOTLAND

The whiskies produced from each of the different geographic regions in Scotland have distinct and identifiable characteristics.

The Highlands
SPEYSIDE

When the Scots refer to the Highlands, they're talking about the upper two-thirds of Scotland. Everything that one associates with Scotland in terms of customs, language, and even plaid comes largely from this region.

The river Spey, which runs through the Highlands, has the greatest concentration of distilleries now in Scotland, hence the subregion known as Speyside. In general, the whiskies from this area tend to be sweet, clean, and rather subtle.

Speyside whiskies vary in weight and express differing intensities and layers of complexity. Some malts have pronounced fruity and honeyed notes, whereas others are bone dry and a bit salty. Still other whiskies exhibit pepper and other exotic spice notes.

The delicate, refined famous whiskies such as the Macallan and the Glenlivet, fruitier and somewhat spicier malts (Knockando and Glenrothes), and whiskies that possess spicier and more powerful characteristics (Mortlach and Aberlour) are all from this region.

THE NORTHERN HIGHLANDS

The whiskies from the Northern Highlands are medium-bodied.
A maritime, salty, seaweedy, and sometimes spicy character pre-
vails. Clynlish and Glen Ord tend toward the spicier and saltier
end of the spectrum. Dalmore and Glenmorangie are a bit richer
and full-bodied.

WESTERN HIGHLANDS

With few distilleries in this region, those such as Ben Nevis,
Glengoyne, Loch Lomond, and Oban share the characteristics of
being full-flavored and possessed with a persistent palate. Creamy
and nutty notes abound. In the case of Oban, there is an obvious
peaty character.

EASTERN HIGHLANDS

The whiskies nearer Edinburgh have fresh and fruity notes and
light to medium body. The distilleries located a bit further south,
in Campbeltown and Islay, are more full-bodied, with chocolate,
toffee, and caramel qualities.

The Campbeltown region was once home to the largest number
of distillers, but, through overproduction and unsavory business
tactics, it became associated with mediocre and cynical whisky
production. Three distilleries are left in Campbeltown at the
moment, and Springbank is the only one producing commercial
quantities of whisky. One of the most highly regarded distilleries
in Scotland, Springbank produces three different malts. Their
flagship bottling is medium-peated, salty, and has some exotic
fruit notes. Longrow is made from heavily peated malt. The third,
Hazelburn, is made from unpeated malt.

Located on the southern coast of Scotland in view of Northern
Ireland, Islay (pronounced eye-lay) produces whiskies that are easily identified because of their intensity and very specific flavor
profile. The distilleries of Lagavulin, Laphroaig, Caol Ila,

1. THE SCOTCH FROM OBAN IS KNOWN FOR ITS PEATY CHARACTERISTICS.

2. THE WHISKIES FROM THE TOWN OF EDINBURGH ARE LIGHTER THAN OTHERS.

3. THE BOWMORE DISTILLERY PRODUCES THE FULL-BODIED SCOTCH FROM ISLAY.

1. ISLE OF MULL IS HOME TO TOBERMORY WHISKY, WHICH CAN BE SALTY BECAUSE [OF ITS] PROXIMITY TO THE SEA.

2. FLOOR MALTINGS, SUCH AS THIS AT THE SPRINGBANK DISTILLERY, ARE FREQUEN[TLY] REPLACED BY DRUM MALTINGS.

Bowmore, Ardbeg, Bruichladdich, and Bunnahabhain all call to mind powerful whiskies that are salty, intense, and reminiscent of the smell of the ocean. For some, their intensity may be a bit too much, but for those serious about their whisky, at least one favorite is likely to come from this region.

THE LOWLANDS

This region is the most industrialized and heavily populated region of Scotland. Lowland whisky was used primarily for blending because of its charm and fresh qualities. Auchentoshen is light-bodied and fresh and tastes of green herbs. Bladnoch is also light and displays a bit more fruit. Glenkinchie has a nose that exhibits floral and grassy notes. All these whiskies share an easy-drinking, fresh, slightly fruity character.

THE ISLANDS OF SKYE, MULL, ORKNEY, ARRAN, AND JURA

The island whiskies share some general attributes. Peppery, smoky, peaty, and salty are some of the traits. But the whiskies from each island have some specific characteristics. The whisky produced in Jura is medium-peated, slightly salty, and mouth coating. Tobermory whisky is made on the small Isle of Mull. It is lighlty peated and a bit sweet. Whiskies from the Arran Isles are the least distinctive in character of all the island whiskies. Talisker is produced on the Isle of Skye. It's a big, powerful whisky that is very spicy and salty. There is a pair of whiskies produced on the Orkney Isles: Highland Park and Scapa. These whiskies have it all: spicy, smoky, spicy, salty, and peaty. Scapa tends to express more of the seaweedy and salty notes; Highland Park has more smoky aromatics.

ONE IN **FIFTY JOBS** IN SCOTLAND IS RELATED TO THE WHISKY INDUSTRY. APPROXIMATELY **18.5 MILLION CASKS** OF WHISKY ARE SLEEPING IN VARIOUS DISTILLERIES ALL OVER SCOTLAND AT THIS MOMENT.

1. OPPOSITE PAGE: THE AUCHENTOSHAN DISTILLERY IS KNOWN FOR THE LIGHT-BODIED WHISKIES OF THE LOWLANDS.

2. SPIRIT SAFES ARE STILL USED BY DISTILLERIES TO ENSURE THE ALCOHOL IS PROPERLY CONTROLLED AND ACCOUNTED FOR.

3. WHISKIES FROM THE ISLE OF JURA CARRY SOME SALTY, PEATY CHARACTERISTICS.

CHAPTER CHAPTER

A SENSE OF PLACE & TASTE

1. BECAUSE OF ITS LOCATION, THE LAPHROAIG DISTILLERY ON ISLAY PRODUCES A VERY BRINY WHISKY.

2. OPPOSITE PAGE: THE CONCENTRATION OF SALT IN THE WATER OF SCOTLAND ADDS A DISTINCT FLAVOR TO ITS WHISKIES.

The French believe in a concept called *terroir*. Generally speaking, the word *terroir* implies the specific attributes of a place, or, to put it another way, a sense of place. The same concept can be applied to the whiskies of Scotland. In France, for example, the Chardonnay grape can be cultivated and turned into wine in any number of locations over the globe, but—say the French—only Le Montrachet can be made to "happen" on that particular 7.5 hectares within the communes of Puligny and Chassagne-Montrachet, in the Côte de Beaune, in the Côte d'Or, and in the region of Burgundy. Applying the same concept to Scotland, *terroir* might explain why Aberlour whisky tastes so different from Tamdhu. Or why Lagavulin and Laphroaig, two distilleries from Islay that are just a stone's throw from each other, produce whiskies that smell and taste as different from each other as do vanilla and licorice.

Although the main ingredients of Scotch whisky are water, barley, peat, and heather, prehistoric geological formation also plays a role in a whisky's flavor. The convergence of resources found in each region undoubtably influences its whisky.

WATER

Scotland has a broad geological array, from sandstone to granite, and traces of minerals and the concentration of salts from the surrounding landscape are measurably present in any given body of local water. The chemicals in the water used to produce a particular whisky must play some role, creating more or less peaty-ness, more or less minerality, etc. Water used in the distilling process is not filtered or adjusted to add or remove any chemical compounds. For example, the water in Islay is very peaty tasting; one would make the assumption that this characteristic is apparent in the whiskies from that region. Some experts say that these flavors survive the distillation process, whereas others tell us that their influence is too subtle to be distinguished in the final product.

BARLEY

Just as the water can make a big difference in flavor, so can the way the barley is malted. How much peat is used, how much exposure the barley has to the smoke, and what other components are mixed in with the peat all affect the flavor. The question of how the type of barley affects flavor is the subject of debate. Other than the sugar content necessary to ensure successful fermentation, does barley possess any more discreet flavor components needed for superior distillation? Most experts say no. A small contingent does insist that the choice of barley type is significant, in particular, the Macallan distillery has been very consistent in its use of a specific barley type, Golden Promise, which they even mention on their Web site.

1. OPPOSITE PAGE: THE MACALLAN DISTILLERY USES ONE SPECIFIC TYPE OF BARLEY IN ITS MALTS.
2. OPPOSITE PAGE: SEAWEED FOUND ALL ALONG THE COAST OF SCOTLAND CONTRIBUTES TO THE SALTINESS FOUND IN SOME WHISKIES.
3. SHOVELING PEAT INTO THE FURNACE—PEAT IS THE FUEL USED FOR HEATING AND DRYING THE BARLEY.

PEAT

For the novice whisky drinker, the flavor of peat is the most obvious and distinctly identifiable quality of malt whisky. Peat is burned in a kiln below the floor where the germinated barley is raked out. The smoke from the burning peat passes through wire mesh above the kiln. This process is used to stop any further germination within the barley and also to impart some flavor. The level of peaty-ness has been declining over the years in most malts, as less experienced consumers find the flavor and aroma a bit off-putting. Adjectives abound: seaweedy, salty, medicinal, smoky, and Band-Aid-like have been used to describe the peat. Like the heather and seaweed that prosper in the Scottish landscape, peat is an intrinsic component of Scotch whisky. Most, but not all, of the most intensely peat-flavored whiskies come from the islands. Whiskies such as Ardbeg, Bowmore, Highland Park, Lagavulin, Laphroaig, and Oban are considered to possess the most pronounced peat component. The Bruichladdich distillery, in Islay, is currently in the process of distilling two new whiskies: Octomore and Port Charlotte, which, when mature, will join the ranks of the most intensely flavored malts. The feeling of many experienced whisky drinkers is that the more intense the peat character, the more authentic the whisky.

HEATHER

Heather is mixed with peat by some whisky makers, mainly by those in Speyside, to use in the malting process. This is said to add a perfumed and honeyed character. Some whiskies that have this character include Balvenie, Glen Elgin, and Dalwhinnie.

The origin of the "seaweed" character of certain island whiskies is somewhat of a mystery. This beguiling component often referred to as salty or "sea air" is favored by some aficionados. The prevailing theory is that the flavor components of seaweed get into the soil and hence the water table through rain and evaporation. In addition, some producers believe that the seaweed character in the maritime air penetrates the aging casks of whisky asleep in their warehouses. Whiskies that have this characteristic are Bunnahabhain, Bruichladdich, Jura, and Scapa.

THE STILL

The role of distillation in the shaping of the specific qualities of single malt whisky is a subject that has always been contentious. One faction believes that since the fundamental process of distillation is mainly consistent from distillery to distillery, the variations that occur are due to the entire combination of elements that go into whisky production, such as the ingredients, the equipment, and the whisky maker. Others believe that very small, sometimes minute, variations in the distillation process itself cause appreciable changes to the final product. First and foremost is the shape and configuration of the still itself. For example, the taller the still, the more delicate the whisky. The reason for this is that as the liquid is heated, almost all of the vapor is retrieved and redistilled. Consequently, most of the very strongly flavored estery compounds are fully processed. An example of a distillery with this kind of still is Glenmorangie. Macallan, on the other hand, famously uses very squat stills. The distillery

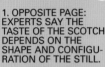

1. OPPOSITE PAGE: EXPERTS SAY THE TASTE OF THE SCOTCH DEPENDS ON THE SHAPE AND CONFIGURATION OF THE STILL.

2. HEATHER IS KNOWN TO ADD A SWEET AND HONEYED FLAVOR TO WHISKY.

3. THE WHISKY AT AUCHENTOSHAN MAKES THREE TRIPS THROUGH THE STILLS.

claims that this configuration is responsible for imparting a rich and oily quality to their malt. Some distillers, such as Bruichladdich and Springbank, use multiple passes through their stills to achieve their unique whiskies.

The mythology surrounding stills is so extreme that whenever a new still is required, whether because of expansion or to replace one no longer functioning, the new still is a replica of the other existing one, down to the patches and dents. Legend has it that at the Linkwood distillery, in Speyside, the manager required that not even a spider's web should be disturbed for fear of corrupting the product.

The whisky is further influenced by the skill of the still man—his sense of just when to draw off the best part of the spirit, his maniacal consistency, and his possession of a nose able to discern 150 or more fragrances from a sample of whisky. Last but not least, the cooperage and aging regimen are critical, but more on this later.

CHAPTER 6

THE SINGLE MALT DIFFERENCE

1. MAGNIFICENT COPPER STILLS HOLD THE WHISKY UNTIL IT'S READY FOR BARRELING.

2. DEWAR'S IS KNOWN FOR HAVING ONE OF THE FIRST BLENDING ROOMS, SHOWN HERE WITH THE FIRST MASTER BREWER.

In the 1850s, Andrew Usher & Co. is reputed to have been the first firm to make a blended whisky, thus launching a new era in the annals of whisky production. By definition, blended whisky is a proportion of malt whisky mixed with grain whisky. Grain whisky is a distillate that can be produced from a number of different grains including corn, wheat, and barley—both the malted (sprouted) and unmalted kinds. Grain whisky is produced in a patent still. This device, invented around 1830, differs from the pot still in that it can operate continuously and does not need to be cleaned and recharged after each pass. While the patent still is tremendously efficient, the distillate that it produces is a largely flavorless, colorless, odorless pure alcohol.

By contrast, single malt Scotch whisky is produced in a pot still from 100 percent malted barley, then aged in oak casks in Scotland for a minimum of three years, after which it has a proof of at least 40 percent alcohol. In addition, single malt Scotch whisky, to be called by that name, must be from a single distillery.

A blend of single malt whiskies—that is, a blend that contains no grain whisky—is called a vatted malt. Though not popular many years ago, there is a renewed interest in marketing this type of product.

Relatively recently, a number of distilleries have introduced single-grain whisky. Single-grain whisky is made from wheat or unmalted (green) barley or corn. Approximately eight distilleries now market single-grain whiskies. Compared with single malt grain whiskies are lighter, drier, and mature earlier. Also, because of the ingredients used, they are cheaper to produce than malts.

In recent years, the growth of the independent bottling sector has been explosive. Many distilleries will sell whisky in cask to private parties. A whisky society or other group of enthusiasts will purchase whisky in cask and then bottle it themselves. These independent bottlers purchase current stock or remaining stocks from mothballed or defunct distilleries, raise the spirit, and bottle it under their own name. For example, you will see the Speymalt series from Macallan bottled by Gordon & MacPhail in a range of ages and vintages, or a 1966 Bowmore 38-year-old single malt Scotch bottled by Duncan Taylor. Generally speaking, independent bottlers concentrate on individual casks, bottle at cask strength (that is, no addition of water to bring down the proof), cold filter, and add no color. These bottlers will also release whisky outside of the normal aging regimen of the distillery bottlings.

1. OPPOSITE PAGE: AN EXAMPLE OF SINGLE-GRAIN WHISKY.
2. OPPOSITE PAGE: BOWMORE'S CASK-STRENGTH WHISKY.
3 AND 4. THE SCOTCH IS EITHER BOTTLED IMMEDIATELY OR LEFT TO AGE IN CASKS.

Depending on the development of this whisky, it may be bottled immediately or allowed to continue aging for bottling at some future date. Besides the Scotch Malt Whisky Society, an organization with an enthusiastic membership worldwide, the two oldest independent bottling concerns are Gordon & MacPhail and Wm. Cadenhead. Other independent bottlers are Adelphi, Blackadder, BDW, Compass Box, Duncan Taylor, Murray McDavid, Scott's Selection, Signatory, the Master of Malt, the Vintage Malt Whisky Co., Whiskies of the World, and Whyte & Whyte, to name a few. These companies bottle and market a number of whiskies that otherwise would most likely never see the light of day. Their goal is to create a bottled whisky that is as close as one can get to a whisky drunk right out of the cask.

When a single malt Scotch is bottled at the distillery, it is generally a combination of several casks of similar age. This ensures a more consistent single malt. Most distilleries practice a cold filtration, so that the whisky will stay clear when it comes into contact with ice. The whisky is then rectified—that is, diluted with a percentage of water to achieve a uniform proof. Most distilleries add coloring so that our expectation of the appearance of the spirit is satisfied. There are pros and cons to these various types of bottlings, but these issues ultimately provide fodder for the endless debate on what makes single malt whisky so compelling a spirit.

THE GREEKS DRINK MORE SCOTCH WHISKY PER CAPITA THAN ANYONE ELSE IN THE WORLD.

AGE BEFORE
BEAUTY

MOST WHISKY IS AGED IN OAK CASKS, SUCH AS THESE AT THE DEWAR'S DISTILLERY IN ABERFELDY.

Before the turn of the century, single malt whisky was drunk pretty much unaged. Collected at the distillery in a barrel, it was sold to a merchant who then bottled it as necessary. Around 1915, a governmental agency was formed to oversee the production of whisky, and it decreed that whisky had to be aged in cask for a minimum of three years before it could be called whisky. Instead of using any old container to hold the collected spirits, distilleries were now compelled to use casks of a higher quality, as three years in a barrel that had previously held pickled fish would have an impact that might not be too nice on the whisky's flavor. Casks that were made from French or American oak and used by Spanish sherry bodegas and Kentucky bourbon producers for aging and ship- ping became the Scotch distillers' vessels of choice. At this point in history, these barrels could be had for nominal prices for a variety of reasons, but mainly because it was cheaper for the owners of the foreign distilleries to sell them at their exportation landing point than to ship them back empty. This turned out to be a boon for the Scots and their whisky, as several attributes of these barrels—whether they were constructed from American or French oak, the degree of char on the inside of the barrel, and the number of "fills" of either sherry or **bourbon that each barrel has experienced—proved to have a very positive effect on the aging of whisky.**

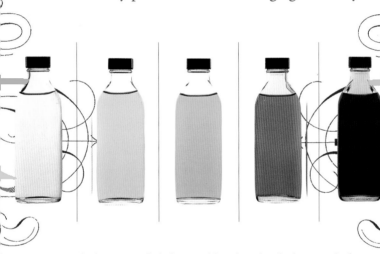

Most whisky is *rectified*, that is, diluted with a little water before it goes into an oak cask. Whisky comes out of the still at around 70 percent alcohol, or 140 proof. It is rectified to approximately 63 percent alcohol when put in cask. At bottling, a further dilution occurs, 40 percent being the normal strength for European Economic Community (EEC) countries, and 43 percent for whisky that is exported. With the growth of the independent bottling market (in which whisky is privately purchased in cask from the distiller and bottled elsewhere), one can also find *cask-strength* bottlings. These range from 43 percent to more than 64 percent. Now many distilleries are experimenting with other types of oak barrels to finish their whisky, including those used in the aging of brandy, port, and rum. In some cases, a whisky will spend eight years in a bourbon barrel—which tends to impart a lighter flavor than, say, a sherry barrel—and finish for six months to a year in a brandy barrel.

1. OPPOSITE PAGE: THE COLOR OF DISTILLED WHISKY DEPENDS ON THE BARRELS IN WHICH IT'S AGED.

2 AND 3. A COOPER CREATES SPECIALTY BARRELS USED FOR THE AGING OF SCOTCH WHISKY.

As whisky ages, an exchange between the liquid inside the barrel and the conditions outside the barrel occurs. Between 2 and 5 percent of the whisky in barrel evaporates into the atmosphere each year. The percentage varies, depending on the humidity in the cellar where the barrels are stored. The poetic name for this costly evaporation is known as the "angel's share." In addition, some feel that the characteristics of the environment in which it is aged can affect the whisky. For example, if the cellar is near the seacoast, the whisky will take on a briny or salty quality.

As whisky remains in its oak cask, it is transformed through the softening action of the oak tannins and other compounds found in the wood, as well as the flavors contained in the wood itself. Residual flavorings of bourbon, sherry, or other liquids leave their marked characteristics.

The actual construction of the barrels can contribute to the whisky's flavor as well. When barrels are being made, the wood is cut into narrow planks called staves. These staves are air-dried for a number of years to rid the wood of its most bitter tannin components. Next the staves are soaked in water. An experienced cooper will then take each stave and, holding it over a fire, bend it into the shape he needs for his barrel. This shaping process "toasts" the surface of the staves that will come in contact with the whisky. The "toast" on a barrel, which can range anywhere from light to extra dark, is therefore another source of flavor. The intensity of this characteristic varies depending on the intensity of the "toastedness" of the barrel.

Most whisky is released having been aged between eight and fifteen years. Common releases are 8-year-old, 10-year-old, 12-year-old, 14-year-old, and 15-year-old. Unless a whisky is from a single cask, in which case it will be identified as such, single malt

THE AGE OF THE WHISKY IS STATED PROMINENTLY ON THE BOTTLE. THESE ARE 10-, 12-, 17-, AND 21-YEAR-OLD BOTTLINGS.

Scotch whisky is the result of combining the contents of a number of casks that are generally, but not always, of the same age and the same distillery. The age stated on a bottle of whisky is the age of the youngest whisky contained in it. On the labels of older, rarer bottlings, one may find the date of distillation, the date of bottling, and an age statement, e.g., 17-year-old, 21-year-old, and so on. When an age statement is given, it is rounded to the lowest complete year that the whisky has been in cask. Sometimes a distillery will choose to quote a younger age statement or not give one at all.

Whisky does not inherently improve with age (just think of some of the people that you know). Certainly some rare, old, expensive whiskies are much greater than their younger counterparts, but this tends to be the exception and not the rule. After twenty-one years, most whiskies begin to lose freshness and take on a rather musty, woody, flat character. Remember, this is just a general guide; some old whiskies are very beautiful. About this question of age, when it comes to whiskey, go out and taste for yourself and discover your own favorites.

CHAPTER **8** CHAPTER

BOTTLING

Interest outside of Scotland in single malt whisky has been increasing since the late 1970s. At the same time sales of blended whisky, while still the highest of the brown spirits, have been falling gradually; in the United States between 1994 and 1999, sales were down by 3.3 percent. But, from 1999 to 2004, there was a steady increase in the sale of whisky in general. Sales for single malts increased by 14 percent for this period. This upward trend shows no sign of abating. Distillers have been taking advantage of this trend by expanding the age range of their bottlings, and independent bottlings have become more readily available. Consequently, at this point in time it is virtually impossible to have a definitive book containing all of the whiskies available in the world, as that number is constantly changing.

This guide to whisky presents you with a general overview including blended, distillery, and independent bottlings. The relative alcoholic strength of the different bottlings, as previously stated, works like this: Distillery bottlings are at 40 percent alcohol (80 proof) when sold in any member country of the EEC, and 43 percent (86 proof) when sold on the export market. Independent bottlings may be sold at "cask" strength. This number can vary from 43 percent (86 proof) to 67 percent (134 proof). Distillery bottlings tend to be much more consistent than independent bottlings. Distilleries will blend various casks of single malt whisky in order to achieve what they feel is the supreme expression of their product. Independent bottlings are from single casks, and these casks exhibit quite a bit of variation from one another. This is by no means a bad thing, but it would be unfair to judge a whisky with just one taste from an independent bottle. It may be most rewarding to compare the distillery's bottling against an independent whenever both samples are available to you. With the exception of certain private society bottlings, the distillery name and age and strength statements are in evidence on the label. In some cases, casks are purchased from defunct distilleries. These independently bottled examples will be the last ever available. Thanks to the efforts of these private societies, the memory of some of the closed distilleries will live on for a while longer.

WHAT'S ON THE LABEL:

SOME DEFINITIONS

For the novice whisky drinker, reading a whisky label can be a daunting task. Once you become familiar with all the terms and phrases used on the label, and have a little tasting experience under your belt, you can get a pretty good idea of what to expect from the contents contained within. The following terms and their meanings are listed in descending order of importance here. Remember, not all terms are included on every label.

TYPES OF WHISKY
Whisky
An alcoholic beverage distilled from malted barley or other types of grains and matured in oak barrels. Whisky is made in a variety of countries all over the globe, but it was originally produced in Scotland and Ireland. *Whiskey* spelled with an *e* refers to the liquid made outside of Scotland. *Whisky* with no *e* refers to the drink made in Scotland (also in Canada, just to further confuse the issue).

Malt Whisky
Made from malted, that is, germinated, barley. Malt whisky is made in single batches.

Single Malt Whisky
Malt whisky made from one individual distillery. Although the majority of malt whisky distilleries are in Scotland, there are a few in other countries as well.

Scotch Whisky
Whisky that is produced in the country of Scotland. The spirit must be aged a minimum of three years.

Single Malt Scotch Whisky
An individual malt whisky that is produced at a distillery in Scotland

Single Cask
Whisky that is bottled from an individual barrel. It's usually the production of an independent bottler.

Grain Whisky

A whisky that is made from a grain other than malted barley, such as wheat, unmalted barley, and corn.

Single-Grain Whisky

Similar to single malt whisky but made using a grain-based spirit. Single-grain whisky is lighter and more neutral than malt whisky.

Blended Scotch Whisky

A mixture of grain whisky and malt whisky. Blended whisky, or Scotch, is by far the most popular type of Scotch that people have sampled. The process for creating blended Scotch whisky is analogous to Champagne, in that the blender's art is to achieve a consistent flavor profile for each individual brand.

Vatted Malt

A blend of malt whiskies from a variety of distillers. Sometimes these are vintage dated if all the whiskies used in the blend come from the same year.

Triple-Distilled Whisky

Processed to the vapor point three times. Traditional production methods use two stills in combination to produce malt whisky. A number of distilleries use three stills in tandem to create a more refined spirit.

PEAT

After the barley has undergone its germination process, heat is used to prevent the barley from further maturation. Peat is burned to create the heat to stop the process and add a distinctly smoky malt whisky flavor. Different distilleries use varying intensities and durations of peat smoke to achieve their desired whisky flavor profile.

WOOD TYPES AND FINISHES

Whisky was traditionally aged in used sherry casks. These barrels, made out of oak, contained sherry and were shipped to the United Kingdom, where they were then refilled by the distilleries with their newly produced malt whisky.

In addition to French oak sherry barrels, American oak barrels originally used for maturing Bourbon whisky are also used for maturing malt whisky.

Some distilleries are now transferring the maturing spirit into other types of wood barrels to finish their aging process. These barrels include ones that have held vintage wines, e.g., red Burgundy, Port, and Madeira. The belief is that the whiskies finished in this manner will have an added degree of complexity.

OTHER LABEL TERMS
Cask Strength

Bottling the mature malt whisky with no rectification, that is, no water has been added to lower the proof results in "cask-strength" whisky. Generally speaking, the proof standard is 80 percent of 40 percent alcohol for whiskies made for export. There are some bottles that are 86 percent of 43 percent alcohol.

Cask strength is the proof that the whisky has attained during its maturation process without ever being diluted with water after the initial barrel-filling process. (Some but not all malts have a small amount of water added before being put in the barrel.)

The goal is to bottle a whisky that will approximate the experience of drinking the malt straight out of the barrel at the distillery. These cask-strength bottlings are generally the product of independent bottlers.

Un-chill-filtered

Bottled without being chilled. Chill filtration is the process of lowering the temperature of the whisky before bottling to prevent the bottled whisky from changing color or becoming cloudy when ice is added to it upon serving. Some argue that this procedure removes some aromatic and flavor components from the finished product. Un-chill-filtered whiskies are considered more pure or natural.

Vintage

Some distilleries produce a vintage bottling in which all the whisky in a particular "edition" comes from a single year. The label will state the year, or *vintage,* instead of making a general age declaration. (Note: In beverage contexts, the word *vintage* does not refer to age or value thereof, only to the fact that all of its kind were bottled in the same year, such as a vintage 2005 whisky.) A recent trend is to release "library" editions of very old single-vintage malts. These are quite expensive.

The Single Malt Brands

SINGLE MALT WHISKY BRANDS

Brands

ABERFELDY
ABERLOUR
ALLT-A-BHANNIE
AN CNOC
ARDBEG
ARDMORE
ARRAN
AUCHENTOSHAN
AUCHROISK
AULTMORE
BALBLAIR
BALMENACH
BALVENIE
BEN NEVIS
BENRIACH
BENRINNES
BENROMACH
BLADNOCH
BLAIR ATHOL
BOWMORE
BRORA
BRUICHLADDICH
BUNNAHABHAIN
CAOL ILA
CAPERDONICH
CARDHU
CLYNELISH
CRAGGANMORE
DALLAS DHU
DAILUAINE
DALMORE
DALWHINNIE
DEANSTON
DRUMGUISH
DUFFTOWN
EDRADOUR
FETTERCAIRN
GLENBURGIE
GLEN DEVERON
GLENDRONACH
GLENDULLAN
GLEN ELGIN
GLENFARCLAS
GLENFIDDICH
GLEN GARIOCH
GLENGOYNE
GLEN GRANT
GLEN KEITH
GLENKINCHIE
THE GLENLIVET
GLENLOSSIE
GLENMORANGIE
GLEN MORAY
GLEN ORD
GLEN ROTHES
GLEN SCOTIA
GLENTAUCHERS
GLENTURRET
HIGHLAND PARK
IMPERIAL
INCHGOWER
ISLE OF JURA
KNOCKANDO
LAGAVULIN
LAPHROAIG
LINKWOOD
LITTLEMILL
LOCH LOMOND (INCHMURRIN & OLD RHOSDHU)
LONGMORN
THE MACALLAN
MANNOCHMORE
MILTONDUFF
MORTLACH
NORTH PORT
OBAN
OLD PULTENEY
PORT ELLEN
ROSEBANK
ROYAL BRACKLA
ROYAL LOCHNAGAR
SCAPA
SPEYBURN
SPEYSIDE
SPRINGBANK
STRATHISLA
TALISKER
TAMDHU
TAMNAVULIN
TEANININCH
TOBERMORY
TOMATIN
TOMINTOUL
TORMORE
TULLIBARDINE

ABERFELDY
HIGHLAND (SOUTHERN)

Built by the sons of the famous blender John Dewar in the 1890s, this distillery is situated in beautiful woodland, which is home to a fine family of red squirrels whose likeness is emblazoned on the Aberfeldy label. Mostly used for blending (Aberfeldy is a major contributor to Dewar's), some is available in both independent and distillery bottlings.

ABERFELDY DISTILLERY

Aberlfeldy
Perthshire PH35 2EB / Scotland
Tel: +44 (0)1887 820330 / Fax: +44 (0)1887 820432
Visitors' center: Yes

REGION: Highland (Southern)

AGE WHEN BOTTLED: 15-year-old

STRENGTH: 43%

INDEPENDENT BOTTLINGS: Blackadder International, Cadenhead, Gordon & MacPhail, Scott's Selection, Signatory

TASTING NOTES:

Aromas: Nutty, fragrant, oaky notes
Flavors: Rich, a bit sweet, smooth finish

ABERLOUR
HIGHLAND (SPEYSIDE)

Aberlour was founded in 1826, but its label reads 1879. This latter date reflects the year the distillery was rebuilt after a devastating fire. Pernod-Ricard, a French conglomerate, now owns the distillery, and, in addition to modernizing the facilities, it has launched a massive advertising push at home. As a result, most of Aberlour's single malt bottlings are sold in France. Much of the distillery's production is used for blending.

ABERLOUR DISTILLERY

Aberlour
Banffshire AB38 9PJ / Scotland
Tel: +44 (0)1340 871204 / Fax: +44 (0)1340 871729
www.aberlour.co.uk
Visitors' center: Yes

REGION: Highland (Speyside)

AGE WHEN BOTTLED: 10-year-old, 21-year-old, 100-year-old, and Antique

STRENGTH: 10-year-old: 40%; 21-year-old and Antique: 43%; 100-year-old: 57%

INDEPENDENT BOTTLINGS: Cadenhead, Whisky Galore

TASTING NOTES:

Aromas: Spicy, hot, grassy, floral

Flavors: Peppery, caramel, toffee, medium to full body, long finish

ABERLOUR

ESTᴰ 1879

ABERLOUR
GLENLIVET
DISTILLERY

SPEYSIDE
MALT AGED
TEN YEARS

SINGLE HIGHLAND MALT
SCOTCH WHISKY

AGED 10 YEARS

750 ml

DISTILLED AND BOTTLED IN SCOTLAND
ABERLOUR GLENLIVET DISTILLERY CO. LTD.
ABERLOUR SPEYSIDE

43%
Alc/Vol

0753

ALLT-A-BHANNIE
HIGHLAND (SPEYSIDE)

Although it is one of the newer distilleries extant, dating from 1975, Allt-A-Bhannie was built in traditional style by the Seagram Company. All of its large (1 million gallons plus) output is used for blending. There are no distillery bottlings.

ALLT-A-BHANNIE DISTILLERY

Glenrinnes
Dufftown
Banffshire AB55 4DB / Scotland
Visitors' center: No

REGION: Highland (Speyside)

AGE WHEN BOTTLED: 12-year-old

STRENGTH: 56%

INDEPENDENT BOTTLINGS: Cadenhead, Ian McLeod

TASTING NOTES:

Aromas: Coffee, toffee, slightly hot

Flavors: A bit smoky, hot, sweetish, a touch sour in the finish

AN CNOC
HIGHLAND (SPEYSIDE)

Not to be confused with Knockando, the distillery Knockdhu produces a single malt called An Cnoc. *Knockdhu* means "black hill" in Gaelic, and *an cnoc* means "the hill." The whisky is used in Haig's blended whisky line. Closed in 1983, the distillery was reopened in 1988. The An Cnoc bottling went into production in 1993.

AN CNOC DISTILLERY

Knock, by Huntly
Aberdeenshire AB5 5LI / Scotland
Tel: +44 (0)1466 771223 / Fax: +44 (0)1466 771359
www.knockdhu.com
Visitors' center: No

REGION: Highland (Speyside)

AGE WHEN BOTTLED: 12-year-old, 21-year-old, 1991 Vintage, 30-year-old

STRENGTH: 12-year-old: 40%; 21-year-old: 57.5%; 1991 Vintage: 48%; 30-year-old: 49.2%

INDEPENDENT BOTTLINGS: Adelphi, Cadenhead

TASTING NOTES:

  Aromas: Fresh, honeyed, slightly smoky nose
  Flavors: A bit sweet, orangey, and spicy

ARDBEG
ISLAY

Prior to 1815, when the distillery was officially recognized by excise officials, this site was used for illicit distilling. Sheltered, with access to lots of peat, barley, and good water, Ardbeg is a perfect example of an island distillery. The bulk of its whisky has been used for blending, but now Ardbeg is also available as single malt from a variety of independent bottlers. A new visitor's center was opened in 1998. Tasting notes refer to a 20-year-old Gordon & MacPhail bottling.

ARDBEG DISTILLERY

Port Ellen
Isle of Islay
Argyllshire PA42 7EB / Scotland
Tel: +44 (0)1496 302244 / Fax: +44 (0)1496 302040
www.ardbeg.com
Visitors' center: Yes

REGION: Islay

AGE WHEN BOTTLED: 10-year-old, 17-year-old, Provenance (distilled 1974, bottled 1998)

STRENGTH: 10-year-old and 17-year-old: 40%; Provenance: 55.8%

INDEPENDENT BOTTLINGS: Adelphi, Blackadder International, Cadenhead, Douglas Laing (Old Malt Cask and Provenance), Gordon & MacPhail, Murray McDavid, Signatory

TASTING NOTES:

Aromas: Earthy, oily, spicy, a bit burnt

Flavors: Strong, salty, woody, quite layered. A whisky for aficionados.

ARDMORE
Highland (Speyside)

One of the largest distilleries in Scotland, Ardmore was built by William Teacher in the 1890s. Expanded and modernized in the 1950s, this distillery produces the whisky that goes into Teacher's blended whisky.

ARDMORE DISTILLERY

Kennethmont
Huntly
Aberdeenshire AB54 4NH / Scotland
Tel: +44 (0)1464 831213
Visitors' center: Yes

REGION: Highland (Speyside)

AGE WHEN BOTTLED: 12-year-old Centenary Bottling

STRENGTH: 40%

INDEPENDENT BOTTLINGS: Cadenhead, Gordon & MacPhail, James MacArthur, Signatory

TASTING NOTES:

  Aromas: A little smoky
  Flavors: Grassy, slight bite

  TWENTY PERCENT OF ALL FOOD AND DRINK EXPORTS FROM THE UNITED KINGDOM ARE SCOTCH WHISKY.

ARRAN
ISLE OF ARRAN

This is Scotland's newest distillery, opened in 1995. It is the first malt to be made on the Isle of Arran in more than 150 years. Staying true to its roots, Isle of Arran Distillers produces a range of whiskies without using peat in the distilling process or caramel for artificial coloring.

ARRAN DISTILLERY

Lochranza
Isle of Arran KA27 8HJ / Scotland
Tel: +44 (0)1770 830264 / Fax: +44 (0)1770 830364
www.arranwhisky.com
Visitors' center: Yes

REGION: Isle of Arran

AGE WHEN BOTTLED: No age declaration

STRENGTH: Single malt: 43%; un-chill-filtered: 46%

INDEPENDENT BOTTLINGS: Signatory, Cadenhead

TASTING NOTES:

Aromas: Light and floral

Flavors: Rich, herbaceous, and perfumed

AUCHENTOSHAN
LOWLAND

The origins of this distillery are a bit sketchy; the earliest record of ownership dates back to 1825. Damaged during World War II, the distillery was later rebuilt and modernized. Located right on the dividing line between Lowland and Highland, the distillery sits on the Lowland side but uses peat and water from the Highland side. Usually whisky is distilled twice, but in the case of Auchentoshan a third trip through the still is added. The resulting very smooth whisky is used as an ingredient in various blended whiskies. Visitors may tour this distillery. Tasting notes refer to the 10-year-old.

AUCHENTOSHAN DISTILLERY

Dalmuir
Dunbartonshire G81 4SG / Scotland
Tel: +44 (0)1389 878561 / Fax: +44 (0)1389 877368
www.auchentoshan.com
Visitors' center: Yes

REGION: Lowland

AGE WHEN BOTTLED: 10-year-old, 21-year-old

STRENGTH: 10-year-old: 40%; 21-year-old: 43%

INDEPENDENT BOTTLINGS: Cadenhead, Duncan Taylor & Co. (cask strength), Signatory

TASTING NOTES:

Aromas: Light, fresh, grassy, lemon

Flavors: Light, clean, citrus, honey, vanilla

AUCHROISK

HIGHLAND (SPEYSIDE)

The owners, International Distillers and Vintners, built the Auchroisk distillery in 1974. Approximately 90 percent of the distillery's output is used for blending. The Singleton, which is a reference to a single cask, is the name of the single malt bottling. The Singleton retains its individuality from the main Auchroisk operation, which can produce up to 1.5 million gallons per year.

SINGLETON AUCHROISK DISTILLERY

Mulben
Banffshire Ab55 3XS / Scotland
Tel: +44 (0)1542 860333 / Fax: +44 (0)1542 860265
Visitors' center: Yes

REGION: Highland (Speyside)

AGE WHEN BOTTLED: 10-year-old

STRENGTH: 40%

INDEPENDENT BOTTLINGS: Cadenhead, Clydesdale, Ian McLeod

TASTING NOTES:

    Aromas: Fresh, fruity, and sweet; a little smoky

    Flavors: Creamy, coffee, and sweet

AULTMORE
HIGHLAND (SPEYSIDE)

Built in the mid-1850s, Aultmore possessed two steam-powered stills until the 1970s, when it doubled in size and modernized its energy source. Originally called the Oban and Aultmore-Glenlivet Distillery, the name was shortened when a map was consulted and it became apparent that Aultmore was a bit distant from the eponymous glen. Most of its production is used for blending.

AULTMORE DISTILLERY

Keith
Banffshire AB55 3QY / Scotland
Tel: +44 (0)1542 882762 / Fax: +44 (0)1542 886467
Visitors' center: No

REGION: Highland (Speyside)

AGE WHEN BOTTLED: 12-year-old

STRENGTH: 43%

INDEPENDENT BOTTLINGS: Adelphi, Cadenhead, Duncan Taylor & Co. (cask strength), Hart Brothers, Signatory

TASTING NOTES:

Aromas: Light, faint nose, bit of fruit

Flavors: Smooth, dry, rather simple, pleasant

PRODUCT OF SCOTLAND

BALBLAIR

Single Highland
Malt Scotch
Whisky   POT STILL

UNBLENDED

750ml   *years old* 10 *years old*   40%alc/vol
(80Proof)

TRADEMARK OF PROPRIETORS
Balblair Distillery Company Ltd
Edderton by Tain

SPECIALLY SELECTED, PRODUCED, MATURED & BOTTLED BY
AND UNDER THE RESPONSIBILITY OF
GORDON & MACPHAIL
ELGIN SCOTLAND REGD. BOTTLER

BALBLAIR
HIGHLAND (SPEYSIDE)

Balblair is one of the oldest distilleries in Scotland, originating between 1750 and 1790. It is located in an area that has seen much whisky production, licensed and otherwise, due to its close proximity to excellent sources of peat and fresh water. Most of Balblair whisky is used for blending, with a high percentage being incorporated into Ballantine's blended Scotch whisky. Tasting notes refer to the 10-year-old.

BALBLAIR DISTILLERY

Edderton
Tain
Ross-shire IV19 1LB / Scotland
Tel: +44 (0)1862 821273
www.balblairdistillery.com
Visitors' center: No

REGION: Highland (Speyside)

AGE WHEN BOTTLED: Elements (no age declaration), 10-year-old, 16-year-old

STRENGTH: Elements, 10-year-old, 16-year-old: 40%

INDEPENDENT BOTTLINGS: Cadenhead, Gordon & MacPhail, Signatory

TASTING NOTES:

Aromas: Smoky, sweet, nutty
Flavors: Clean, a bit simple, smoky finish

BALMENACH
HIGHLAND (SPEYSIDE)

Recently reopened by Inver House Distilleries in 1997, Balmenach was a major contributor to Johnnie Walker. The new owners have released two older bottlings in a limited edition. Many independent bottlings are available.

BALMENACH DISTILLERY

Cromdale
Moray PH26 3PF / Scotland
Tel: +44 (0)1479 872569 / Fax: +44 (0)1479 873829
www.balmenachdistillery.com
Visitors' center: No

REGION: Highland (Speyside)

AGE WHEN BOTTLED: 27-year-old (bottled 2001), 28-year-old (1972 vintage)

STRENGTH: 27-year-old: 46%; 28-year-old: 46%

INDEPENDENT BOTTLINGS: Blackadder, Cadenhead, Chieftain's Choice (Ian McLeod & Co.), Cooper's Choice, Gordon & MacPhail, Hart Brothers, Scott's, Whyte & Whyte

TASTING NOTES:

  Aromas: Sweet, exotic fruit
  Flavors: Rich, orange and honey

BALVENIE
HIGHLAND (SPEYSIDE)

Built by William Grant in the 1890s, this distillery stands next to Glenfiddich. Balvenie still has its own maltings and also shares a steam heat source with its more famous neighbor, presumably in exchange for some barrels of Balvenie. Tasting notes refer to 12-year-old.

BALVENIE DISTILLERY

Dufftown
Banffshire AB55 4DH / Scotland
Tel: +44 (0)1340 820373 / Fax: +44 (0)1340 820805
www.balvenie.com
Visitors' center: No

REGION: Highland (Speyside)

AGE WHEN BOTTLED: 10-year-old and 12-year-old "Double Wood," 15-year-old "Single Barrel"

STRENGTH: 10-year-old: 40%; 12-year-old: 40%; 15-year-old: 50.4%

INDEPENDENT BOTTLINGS: Signatory (1974 Vintage, released in 1990)

TASTING NOTES:

Aromas: Floral, high-toned nose
Flavors: Rich hints of honey, a long layered finish

BEN NEVIS
HIGHLAND (WESTERN)

Ben Nevis was founded by "Long John" Macdonald in 1825. It was passed to generations of the Macdonald family until it was bought by a subsidiary of Seager, Evans & Whitbread & Co., Ltd. in 1981. The changing of hands ceased after a continuous still and four pot stills were added. Finally, Ben Nevis was sold to Nikka, a Japanese company, in 1989.

BEN NEVIS DISTILLERY

Loch Bridge
Fort William PH33 6TJ / Scotland
Tel: +44 (0)1397 702476 / Fax: +44 (0)1397 702768
Visitors' center: Yes

REGION: Highland (Western)

AGE WHEN BOTTLED: 10-year-old, 26-year-old

STRENGTH: 10-year-old: 46%; 26-year-old: 54.2%

INDEPENDENT BOTTLINGS: Blackadder, Cadenhead, International, Signatory, SMWS

TASTING NOTES:

   Aromas: Fruity and peaty
   Flavors: Full, nutty, earthy, and peaty

BENRIACH
HIGHLAND

Founded in the 1890s, Benriach had a short life. The distillery closed in 1900 and remained shut for more than half a century. Since reopening in 1965, a large portion of its production goes toward blending and a smaller part is independently bottled.

BENRIACH DISTILLERY

By Elgin
Morayshire IV30 3SJ / Scotland
Tel: +44 (0)1542 783400 / Fax: +44 (0)1542 783404
Visitors' center: By appointment only

REGION: Highland

AGE WHEN BOTTLED: 10-year-old

STRENGTH: 43%

INDEPENDENT BOTTLINGS: Adelphi, Blackadder International, Cadenhead, Duncan Taylor (cask strength), Gordon & MacPhail (Connoisseurs Choice), Whisky Galore

TASTING NOTES:

Aromas: Fruity, spicy, hot
Flavors: Sweet, peach, caramel, lighter finish

BENRINNES
HIGHLAND (SPEYSIDE)

Benrinnes Distillery was first established in 1826.
Mainly used for blending, the first official single
malt bottling at this distillery was in 1991.
Benrinnes is one of the few distilleries to use a
rare triple-distillation process.

BENRINNES DISTILLERY

Aberlour
Banffshire AB38 9NN / Scotland
Tel: +44 (0)1340 871215 / Fax: +44 (0)1340 871840
Visitors' center: No

REGION: Highland (Speyside)

AGE WHEN BOTTLED: 15-year-old

STRENGTH: 43%

INDEPENDENT BOTTLINGS: Blackadder, Hart Brothers,
Signatory

TASTING NOTES:

Aromas: Sherried, smoky nose

Flavors: Rich, full-bodied, tobacco

BENROMACH
HIGHLAND (SPEYSIDE)

Since its inception in 1898, Benromach has
changed ownership more than a few times.
In 1983, DCL, the owner at the time, shut a
number of distilleries in its portfolio, including
Benromach. The distillery was purchased in
1992 by Gordon & MacPhail and officially
reopened in 1998 by the Prince of Wales.
Benromach has a reputation for producing a
clean, medium-peated, lighter style of
Highland whisky.

BENROMACH DISTILLERY & MALT WHISKY CENTRE

Invererne Road
Forres
Morayshire IV36 0EB / Scotland
Tel: +44 (0)1309 675968 / Fax: +44 (0)1343 540155
www.benromach.com
Visitors' center: Yes

REGION: Highland (Speyside)

AGE WHEN BOTTLED: 18-year-old, Vintage 1973

STRENGTH: 18-year-old: 40%; 1973: 40%

INDEPENDENT BOTTLINGS: Cadenhead, Gordon & MacPhail (Connoisseurs Choice), Hart Brothers,

TASTING NOTES:

Aromas: Sweet on the nose; a little smoky and peaty

Flavors: Nutty, exotic spice, cinnamon

BLADNOCH

LOWLAND

The southernmost of all distilleries, Bladnoch has been opened and closed a number of times during its long history. The final closing occurred in 1994, and the site is now used as a tourist center. Since 2000 the distillery is once again in production, albeit in a quite limited fashion.

BLADNOCH

Wigtownshire DG8 9AB / Scotland
Tel: +44 (0)1988 402235
www.bladnoch.co.uk
Visitors' center: Yes

REGION: Lowland

AGE WHEN BOTTLED: 10-year-old

STRENGTH: 43%

INDEPENDENT BOTTLINGS: Adelphi, Cadenhead, Gordon & MacPhail, Signatory

TASTING NOTES:

Aromas: Smoky, caramel, oily

Flavors: Heavy, peaty, tangy, rich

BLAIR ATHOL
HIGHLAND

Established in 1798 in the town of Pitlochry, Blair Athol is one of the oldest working distilleries in Scotland. The output of Blair Athol is mainly used for blending, most notably in Bell's. The distillery also produces a 12-year-old single malt whisky with a strong fruit flavor and a smooth finish. Blair Athol is a model distillery for visiting.

BLAIR ATHOL DISTILLERY

Perth Road
Pitlochry
Perthshire PH16 5LY / Scotland
Tel: +44 (0)1796 482003 / Fax: +44 (0)1796 482001
Visitors' center: Yes

REGION: Highland

AGE WHEN BOTTLED: 12-year-old, 1981 Vintage (bottled 1997)

STRENGTH: 12-year-old: 43%; 1981: 55.5%

INDEPENDENT BOTTLINGS: Cadenhead, Douglas Laing, Signatory

TASTING NOTES:

  Aromas: Black tea and heather

  Flavors: Spicy and very balanced

The oldest distillery on this island, Bowmore was established in 1779. Long owned by Morrison Bowmore Distillers, whose holdings include Auchentoshan and Glen Garioch, Bowmore was sold in 1997 to Suntory of Japan. Even before that sale, however, much of this whisky went to Japan. Bowmore malts most of its own barley. The traditional malting barns with pagoda-shaped ventilators on their roofs now have a new Far Eastern resonance. Tasting notes refer to the 17-year-old. Bowmore bottles a line with evocative names like Surf, Dusk, and Voyage. The Black Bowmore bottling is highly collectable.

BOWMORE DISTILLERY

Isle of Islay
Argyllshire PA43 7GS / Scotland
Tel: +44 (0)1496 810441 / Fax: +44 (0)1496 810757
www.bowmore.com
Visitors' center: Yes

REGION: Islay

AGE WHEN BOTTLED: Legend (no age declaration), Surf (no age declaration), cask strength (no age declaration), 12-year-old, 17-year-old, 21-year-old

STRENGTH: Legend: 40%; Surf: 43%; cask strength: 56%; 12-year-old, 17-year-old, 21-year-old: all 43%

INDEPENDENT BOTTLINGS: Blackadder International, Duncan Taylor & Co., Murray McDavid, SMWS, Signatory, Whisky Galore

TASTING NOTES:

Aromas: Musky, earthy, nutty aromas; beautiful rich color
Flavors: Dry, charcoal, moderate peat, smoky, a touch bitter, very complex

BRORA
HIGHLAND (SPEYSIDE)

Brora distillery was founded in 1819 and was situated next to the Brora coalfield, which provided ready power for the distilling process. In 1896, James Ainslie & Co. took over Brora and rebuilt the distillery just a mile from its original site. DCL then acquired a large holding in Brora, the Clynelish Distillery Co. was formed, and Brora was renamed Clynelish ("klyn-leesh"). In 1925, DCL gained complete control and built a new malt whisky distillery next to Clynelish called Brora that operated until 1968. Brora was closed in 1983 and transformed into a tourist attraction (see Clynelish, page 89).

REGION: Highland (Speyside)

AGE WHEN BOTTLED: 30-year-old (bottled 2003)

STRENGTH: 55.2%

INDEPENDENT BOTTLINGS: Douglas Laing, Signatory

TASTING NOTES:

Aromas: Sweet, vanilla

Flavors: Clean, fresh, fruity

BRUICHLADDICH
ISLAY

Bruichladdich was built right on the sea. It was closed in 1995 and bought by a small group of whisky experts in 2000. They have refurbished the distillery and kept it old-fashioned. The current bottlings are stylistically fresh, light, and quite pure with light to medium peat. All bottlings are un-chill-filtered and unfiltered. Islay spring water is used to rectify the malt to 46 percent. This is possible because Bruichladdich is one of the few distilleries with its own bottling line. The distillery will be producing a range called Port Charlotte and another called Octomore. These ranges will be much more heavily peated whiskies than Bruichladdich. In February 2006, Bruichladdich quadruple-distilled a malt that was approximately 90 percent alcohol, or 180 proof. This production came under the scrutiny of the US Secret Service. The agency was quoted as saying this malt "was a small tweak from being a chemical weapon."

BRUICHLADDICH DISTILLERY

Isle of Islay
Argyllshire PA49 7UN / Scotland
Tel: +44 (0)1496 850221 / Fax: +44(0)1496 850447
www.bruichladdich.com
Visitors' center: Yes

REGION: Islay

AGE WHEN BOTTLED: 10-year-old, 15-year-old, 17-year-old, 20-year-old, 1984 Vintage

STRENGTH: 10-year-old, 17-year-old, 20-year-old, 1984: all 46%

INDEPENDENT BOTTLINGS: Adelphi, Blackadder, Cadenhead, Duncan Taylor & Co. (cask strength), Gordon & MacPhail, Murray McDavid, Scott's, Signatory, SMWS

TASTING NOTES:

  Aromas: Nutty, sweet, light, a touch peaty
  Flavors: Mellow, lightly smoky, a bit sweet, complex, rich finish

aged 12 years

"Westering Home..."

Bunnahabhain
SINGLE ISLAY MALT SCOTCH WHISKY
PRODUCT OF SCOTLAND
THE BUNNAHABHAIN DISTILLERY COMPANY,
BUNNAHABHAIN, ISLE OF ISLAY, SCOTLAND. BOTTLED IN SCOTLAND.

43% alc/vol

Sole U.S.A. Distributor,
Rémy Amérique, Inc.,
New York, N.Y.

750 ml

BUNNAHABHAIN

ISLAY

Bunnahabhain means the "mouth of the river" in Gaelic. This distillery, situated on the northeast coast of Islay, produces a moderately "iodiney" style of Islay whisky. Bunnahabhain is used for blending in the Famous Grouse.

BUNNAHABHAIN DISTILLERY

Port Askaig
Isle of Islay
Argyllshire PA46 7RR / Scotland
Tel: +44 (0)1496 840646 / Fax: +44 (0)1496 840248
Visitors' center: Yes

REGION: Islay

AGE WHEN BOTTLED: 12-year-old

STRENGTH: 43%

INDEPENDENT BOTTLINGS: Blackadder, Duncan Taylor & Co. (cask strength), Gordon & MacPhail, Murray McDavid, Signatory, SMWS

TASTING NOTES:

Aromas: Floral and fresh, with touches of hazelnut and earth

Flavors: Smoky, peppery, hint of wood, a distinct coffee note

CAOL ILA
ISLAY

Caol Ila is Gaelic for "sound of Islay." This distillery was completely rebuilt in the early 1970s. Almost all of the whisky is used for blending. Since 1989, distillery bottlings have been available, as well as numerous independent bottlings. The different styles of malt produced by the distillery can be found in the independent bottlings. Tasting notes refer to a 12-year-old Gordon & MacPhail bottling.

CAOL ILA DISTILLERY

Port Askaig
Isle of Islay
Argyllshire PA46 7RL / Scotland
Tel: +44 (0)1496 840207 / Fax: +44 (0)1496 840660
www.malts.com
Visitors' center: Yes

REGION: Islay

AGE WHEN BOTTLED: 12-year-old, 18-year-old, cask strength (no age declaration)

STRENGTH: 12-year-old: 43%; 18-year-old: 43%; cask strength: 55%

INDEPENDENT BOTTLINGS: Adelphi, Cadenhead, Gordon & MacPhail, Ian McLeod, Murray McDavid, Signatory, Whisky Galore

TASTING NOTES:

Aromas: Earthy, peaty, a touch grassy
Flavors: Earthy, salty, smoky, longish finish

CAPERDONICH

HIGHLAND (SPEYSIDE)

Originally called Glen Grant 2, the distillery was built in 1897 as an adjunct to Glen Grant. The new facility's production was piped into Glen Grant until the turn of the century. The distillery was closed until 1965, when it was expanded and renamed Caperdonich. Never produced as a single malt, all of Caperdonich's output is used in blending. Independent bottlings are available.

CAPERDONICH DISTILLERY

Rothes
Morayshire AB38 7BN
Tel: +44 (0)1542 783300
Visitors' center: No

REGION: Highland (Speyside)

AGE WHEN BOTTLED: 16-year-old

STRENGTH: 40%

INDEPENDENT BOTTLINGS: Duncan Taylor & Co., Gordon & MacPhail, Signatory

TASTING NOTES:

  Aromas: Chocolate, caramel, and burnt sugar aroma

  Flavors: Sweet, woody, a bit of smoke on the palate

 THE FRENCH BUY MORE SCOTCH WHISKY IN ONE MONTH THAN THEY BUY COGNAC IN ONE YEAR.

CARDHU
HIGHLAND (SPEYSIDE)

Cardhu means "black rock" in Gaelic. An old distillery, modernized in the 1960s, the bulk of its whisky is used in Johnnie Walker Black and Red Label blends. On its own, Cardhu is light in color and shows hardly any peat character. A very successful single malt, Cardhu has introduced Cardhu Pure Malt, a vatted whisky, to supply its worldwide demand.

CARDHU DISTILLERY

Knockando
Aberlour
Banffshire AB38 7RY / Scotland
Tel: +44 (0)1346 810204 / Fax: +44 (0)1340 810491
www.malts.com
Visitors' center: No

REGION: Highland (Speyside)

AGE WHEN BOTTLED: 12-year-old, 27-year-old cask strength (distilled 1973)

STRENGTH: 12-year-old: 40%; 27-year-old: 60%

INDEPENDENT BOTTLINGS: Signatory

TASTING NOTES:

  Aromas: Light, faintly earthy, citrus
  Flavors: Fresh, lively, a touch of wood and smoke

CLYNELISH
HIGHLAND (NORTHERN)

Clynelish originally opened in 1819 as a brewery and was converted to a distillery soon after. This distillery was originally named Brora (see page 82), but in 1912, because of a change of ownership, it was renamed Clynelish. In 1925, another distillery was built next door and given the old name of Brora. In 1969, Clynelish reopened in the former mash house of Brora. Its production from the mash house was stenciled as "Brora" on the casks but sold under the name of Clynelish. Almost all of the production is blended into Johnnie Walker Gold.

CLYNELISH DISTILLERY

Brora
Sutherland KW9 6LB / Scotland
Tel: +44 (0)1408 621444 / Fax: +44 (0)1408 621131
Visitors' center: Yes

REGION: Highland (Northern)

AGE WHEN BOTTLED: 14-year-old

STRENGTH: 46%

INDEPENDENT BOTTLINGS: Adelphi, Gordon & MacPhail, Hart Brothers, Ian McLeod, Murray McDavid, Signatory, Whisky Galore

TASTING NOTES:

  Aromas: Peaty, medicinal, smoky
  Flavors: Smoke, heavy peat

CRAGGANMORE
HIGHLAND (SPEYSIDE)

This distillery was established in 1869 by the very experienced John Smith. Mr. Smith had managed several distilleries, including Macallan and Glenlivet, prior to striking out on his own. The distillery was one of the first to make use of a nearby railway link, perhaps one of the reasons that the bulk of the production has always been used for blending. In recent years, this whisky has become one of the United Distillers' Classic Malts and, as such, is now widely available. The stills used are quite old-fashioned in their design.

CRAGGANMORE DISTILLERY

Ballindalloch
Banffshire AB37 9AB / Scotland
Tel: +44 (0)1807 500202 / Fax: +44 (0)1807 500288
www.malts.com
Visitors' center: Yes

REGION: Highland (Speyside)

AGE WHEN BOTTLED: 12-year-old

STRENGTH: 40%

INDEPENDENT BOTTLINGS: Gordon & MacPhail

TASTING NOTES:

  Aromas: Dry, a little hot, smoky, hint of fruit
  Flavors: Medium to heavy body, long, spicy, a bit of vanilla

DAILUAINE
HIGHLAND (SPEYSIDE)

The output of this distillery was mainly used for blending into Johnnie Walker, until the release of a single malt bottling in 1991. Since then Dailuaine has bottled a range of Cask Strength Limited Edition.

DAILUAINE DISTILLERY

Aberlour
Banffshire AB38 7RE / Scotland
Tel: +44 (0)1340 810361 / Fax: +44 (0)1340 810510
Visitors' center: No

REGION: Highland (Speyside)

AGE WHEN BOTTLED: 16-year-old, 22-year-old (distilled 1973), 1980 (bottled 1997)

STRENGTH: 16-year-old: 40%; 22-year-old: 60.92%; 1980: 63%

INDEPENDENT BOTTLINGS: Gordon & MacPhail

TASTING NOTES:

Aromas: Perfumed, sweet
Flavors: Fruity, dry, hot, long finish

DALLAS DHU
HIGHLAND (SPEYSIDE)

Closed for business now, this distillery is run as a tourist attraction. Visit it to see what things were like around the turn of the century. Various independent bottlings from old casks are available, although not too readily. Tasting notes refer to 12-year-old.

DALLAS DHU

Forres
Morayshire IV36 2RR / Scotland
Tel: +44 (0)1309 676548
Visitors' center: Yes

REGION: Highland (Speyside)

AGE WHEN BOTTLED: NA

STRENGTH: NA

INDEPENDENT BOTTLINGS: Cooper's Choice, Gordon & MacPhail, Murray McDavid, Signatory

TASTING NOTES:

Aromas: Hot, oily, nutty, earthy, mushroomy

Flavors: Earthy, woody, syrupy mouth feel, caraway, citrus, intense

DALMORE
Highland (Speyside)

This distillery was founded in 1839 and operated continuously until World War I. At that time the facility was retooled for the production of naval mines. Modernized in 1966, it continues to use several of the stills dating back to 1874. Most of its output goes for blending.

DALMORE DISTILLERY

Alness
Ross-shire IV17 0UT / Scotland
Tel: +44 (0)1349 882362 / Fax: +44 (0)1349 883655
www.thedalmore.com
Visitors' center: Yes

REGION: Highland (Speyside)

AGE WHEN BOTTLED: 12-year-old, Cigar Malt (no age declaration), 21-year-old (distilled 1978), 50-year-old

STRENGTH: 12-year-old: 40%; Cigar Malt: 40%; 50-year-old: 52.6%

INDEPENDENT BOTTLINGS: Cadenhead, Whiskies of the World

TASTING NOTES:

Aromas: Soft, fruity, light nose

Flavors: Full, a bit peaty, smooth, rich finish

DALWHINNIE
HIGHLAND

Gaelic for "meeting place," Dalwhinnie is situated on a rail spur, with abundant peat and fresh water sources and the highest elevation of any distillery in Scotland. Built in 1897, the distillery went through a variety of bankruptcies, purchases, and fires until it finally stabilized in 1938. Although most of its output is used for blending, this malt is now available as part of the Classic Malt series.

DALWHINNIE DISTILLERY

Dalwhinnie
Inverness-shire PH39 1AB / Scotland
Tel: +44 (0)1528 522240
www.malts.com
Visitors' center: Yes

REGION: Highland

AGE WHEN BOTTLED: 15-year-old

STRENGTH: 43%

INDEPENDENT BOTTLINGS: Cadenhead, Gordon & MacPhail

TASTING NOTES:

 Aromas: Light, fresh, a hint of peat

 Flavors: A bit sweet, floral, honeyed, medium length

7 YEAR OLD The Deanston SINGLE HIGHLAND MALT whisky has a smooth, lightly peated, medium flavour which is easy on the palate and leaves a pleasant sweet after-taste. The UNIQUE character is derived from the waters of the RIVER TEITH whose source is high up in the TROSSACHS

SCOTCH WHISKY

THE DEANSTON

Single Highland Malt

750ml

DISTILLED AND MATURED BY DEANSTON DISTILL

PRODUCED and BOTTLED in SC

DEANSTON

Deanston was founded in 1965, which makes this distillery a relative newcomer. It sits on the site of an old textile mill and is named after a nearby town. The new owners use unpeated barley for the whisky. Tasting notes refer to 17-year-old.

DEANSTON DISTILLERY

Near Doune
Perthshire FK16 6AG / Scotland
Tel: +44 (0)1786 841422 / Fax: +44 (0)1786 841439
Visitors' center: No

REGION: Highland (Southern)

AGE WHEN BOTTLED: 12-year-old, 17-year-old

STRENGTH: 12-year-old: 40%; 17-year-old: 40%

INDEPENDENT BOTTLINGS: Signatory

TASTING NOTES:

  Aromas: Nutty and vanilla aromas
  Flavors: Smoky, nutty, sweetish finish

DRUMGUISH
HIGHLAND (SPEYSIDE)

Drumguish is the 5-year-old single malt produced at the Speyside distillery (see page 162). The Speyside distillery was built across the road from the site of the original Drumguish distillery, which was closed in 1911. The first distillation at the Speyside distillery was in 1991. In addition to Drumguish, a 12-year-old single malt called Speyside is produced as well.

THE SPEYSIDE DISTILLERY

Glen Yromie
Kingussie
Inverness-shire PH21 1NS / Scotland
Tel: +44 (0)1540 661060 / Fax: +44 (0)1540 661959
www.speyside.com
Visitors' center: No

REGION: Highland (Speyside)

AGE WHEN BOTTLED: Drumguish (no age declaration); Speyside: 12-year-old

STRENGTH: Drumguish: 40%; Speyside: 43%

INDEPENDENT BOTTLINGS: None

TASTING NOTES:

  Aromas: Perfumed, nutty
  Flavors: Sweet, floral, dry

DUFFTOWN
HIGHLAND (SPEYSIDE)

The town of Dufftown has a longstanding reputation for producing some of the finest whisky in Scotland. Dufftown Distillery is another whose owners felt compelled, like so many of their neighbors, to add Glenlivet to its name. The distillery was built in 1887 and purchased by the famous blenders Arthur Bell & Sons in 1933. Since then, most of this whisky has gone into a variety of Bell's blends. In 1974, Bell built a sister distillery, called Pittvaich-Glenlivet, for Dufftown. The idea was to increase production without compromising quality. The new distillery copied down to the last detail the pot stills from Dufftown-Glenlivet.

DUFFTOWN DISTILLERY

Dufftown
Keith
Banffshire AB55 4BR / Scotland
Tel: +44 (0)1340 820224 / Fax: +44 (0)1340 820060
Visitors' center: No

REGION: Highland (Speyside)

AGE WHEN BOTTLED: 15-year-old

STRENGTH: 43%

INDEPENDENT BOTTLINGS: Cadenhead, Murray McDavid, Signatory, Whisky Galore

TASTING NOTES:

Aromas: Fruity, with notes of apple and pear
Flavors: Lightish, clean, fresh, a bit floral

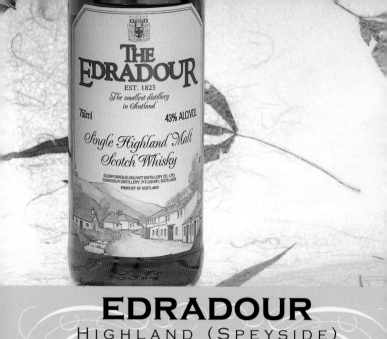

EDRADOUR
HIGHLAND (SPEYSIDE)

Edradour, the smallest distillery in Scotland, functions as if it were still operating in the nineteenth century. The entire enterprise is run by four people, and almost everything is done by hand. Appointments for tours are necessary, and if you want to travel back in time, Edradour is a good place to visit. Edradour was first bottled as a single malt in 1986.

EDRADOUR DISTILLERY

Pitlochry
Perthshire PH36 5JP / Scotland
Tel: +44 (0)1796 473524 / Fax: +44 (0)1796 472002
www.edradour.co.uk
Visitors' center: By appointment only

REGION: Highland (Speyside)

AGE WHEN BOTTLED: 10-year-old

STRENGTH: 40%

INDEPENDENT BOTTLINGS: Gordon & MacPhail, Signatory

TASTING NOTES:

   Aromas: Spicy, hot, earthy nose
   Flavors: Peppery, peaty, smoky, hints of tobacco and caramel

FETTERCAIRN

Fettercairn has been producing whisky since at least 1824. According to one source, Sir John Gladstone, father of William Gladstone, three-time prime minister of Britain (1868–74, 1880–86, 1892–94), was once chairman of the board of this distillery. Prime Minister Gladstone, who enacted numerous reforms throughout his political career, was instrumental in allowing bottled whisky to be sold to the general population. Almost all of Old Fettercairn is used in blending.

FETTERCAIRN DISTILLERY

Laurencekirk
Kincardineshire AB30 1YE / Scotland
Tel: +44 (0)1561 340244 / Fax: +44 (0)1561 340447
Visitors' center: Yes

REGION: Highland

AGE WHEN BOTTLED: 10-year-old

STRENGTH: 40%

INDEPENDENT BOTTLINGS: Gordon & MacPhail, Signatory

TASTING NOTES:

Aromas: Melon, banana
Flavors: Honeyed, banana, sweet

GLENBURGIE
HIGHLAND (SPEYSIDE)

Reported to have been established in 1810, Glenburgie is used mainly as a blending component for Ballantine's. The year 2002 saw the release of a 15-year-old single malt. The more familiar bottlings are all independent.

GLENBURGIE DISTILLERY

By Alves
Forres
Morayshire IV36 0QY / Scotland
Tel: +44 (0)1343 850258 / Fax: +44 (0)1343 850480
Visitors' center: No

REGION: Highland (Speyside)

AGE WHEN BOTTLED: 15-year-old

STRENGTH: 46%

INDEPENDENT BOTTLINGS: Cadenhead, Duncan Taylor & Co. (cask strength), Gordon & MacPhail, Hart Brothers, Signatory, SMWS

TASTING NOTES:

   Aromas: Sweet and candied
   Flavors: Toffee, oily, a bit dry

SCOTCH WHISKY EXPORTS GENERATED 2.24 BILLION POUNDS FOR THE UNITED KINGDOM IN 2004.

GLEN DEVERON
Highland (Speyside)

Mostly used for blending, the offerings from this distillery often find their way into William Lawson's. The independent bottlings take their name from the distillery and are labeled MacDuff.

MACDUFF DISTILLERY

Banff
Banffshire AB4 3JT / Scotland
Tel: +44 (0)1261 812612 / Fax: +44 (0)1261 818083
Visitors' center: No

REGION: Highland (Speyside)

AGE WHEN BOTTLED: 10-year-old

STRENGTH: 40%

INDEPENDENT BOTTLINGS: Cadenhead, Duncan Taylor & Co. (cask strength), Gordon & MacPhail, Signatory

TASTING NOTES:

Aromas: Sweet, sherry
Flavors: Fresh, slight smokiness

GLENDRONACH
HIGHLAND (SPEYSIDE)

Traditional elements such as floor maltings and coal-fired stills abound, even though the distillery was modernized and expanded in the late 1960s. Much of this whisky goes into the blended Scotch Teacher's. Tasting notes refer to 12-year-old sherry cask.

GLENDRONACH DISTILLERY

Forgue
Aberdeenshire AB54 6DA / Scotland
Tel: +44 (0)1466 730202 / Fax: +44 (0)1466 730313
Visitors' center: Yes

REGION: Highland (Speyside)

AGE WHEN BOTTLED: 12-year-old, Tradition (12-year-old, matured in both bourbon barrel and sherry cask), Original (12-year-old matured in sherry cask), 15-year-old (matured in sherry cask), 18-year-old

STRENGTH: All 12-year-olds: 40%; 15-year-old: 40%; 18-year-old: 43%

INDEPENDENT BOTTLINGS: Signatory, Whisky Galore

TASTING NOTES:

Aromas: Fruity, sweet, nutty citrus—orange peel
Flavors: Toffee, coffee, smoky, caramel finish

GLENDULLAN
SPEYSIDE

Once the favorite of King Edward VII, Glendullan dates back to 1897. It's used as a component for Old Parr. The malt is also a component in the vatted version of Cardhu.

GLENDULLAN DISTILLERY

Dufftown
Keith
Banffshire AB55 4DJ / Scotland
Tel: +44 (0)1340 820250 / Fax: +44 (0)1340 820064
Visitors' center: No

REGION: Speyside

AGE WHEN BOTTLED: 12-year-old

STRENGTH: 43%

INDEPENDENT BOTTLINGS: Cadenhead, Signatory, SMWS

TASTING NOTES:

    Aromas: Light, perfumed
    Flavors: Dry, slightly fruity

GLEN ELGIN
Highland (Speyside)

This whisky is very difficult to find because it is in great demand as a high-quality blending malt. Mostly used for blending in White Horse in the past, the distillery bottles a 12-year-old single malt now too.

GLEN ELGIN DISTILLERY

Longmor
Elgin
Morayshire IV30 3SL / Scotland
Tel: +44 (0)1343 860212 / Fax: +44 (0)1343 862077
www.malts.com
Visitors' center: No

REGION: Highland (Speyside)

AGE WHEN BOTTLED: 12-year-old

STRENGTH: 43%

INDEPENDENT BOTTLINGS: Hart Brothers, Murray McDavid, Signatory, Whisky Galore

TASTING NOTES:

  Aromas: Sweet, floral, smoky
  Flavors: Sweet and honeyed, fresh finish

GLENFARCLAS
HIGHLAND (SPEYSIDE)

For five generations, the Grant family has privately owned this distillery. Modernized twice, first in the 1960s and again in the 1980s, Glenfarclas is a large, up-to-date facility. As the first distillery to commercially bottle "cask-strength" whisky, Glenfarclas started a trend that has become de rigueur for single malt enthusiasts. Glenfarclas now ages all its spirits exclusively in sherry casks. The freshness and bite of young whisky in the 12-year-old, the complexity and balance of the 15-year-old, and the Cognac- or Madeira-like qualities of the 25-year-old are perfect examples of what happens as whisky ages.

GLENFARCLAS DISTILLERY

Ballindalloch
Banffshire AB37 9BD / Scotland
Tel: +44 (0)1807 500245 / Fax: +44 (0)1807 500234
www.glenfarclas.co.uk
Visitors' center: Yes

REGION: Highland (Speyside)

AGE WHEN BOTTLED: 10-year-old, 12-year-old, 15 year
old-year-old, 21-year-old, 25-year-old; "105" (cask strength, no
age declaration)

STRENGTH: 10-year-old: 40%; 12-, 21-, and 25-year-old: all
43%; 15-year-old: 46%, "105": 60%

INDEPENDENT BOTTLINGS: Cadenhead

TASTING NOTES:

Aromas: 12-year-old: nutty, grassy; 15-year-old: floral, nutty,
grassy; 21-year-old: fruity, sweet, vanilla, nutty; 25-year-old:
fruity, oily, earthy, nutty; "105": intense and spicy

Flavors: 12-year-old: sweet, light, simple; 15-year-old: hot,
very long, woody, a bit smoky; 21-year-old: smoky, quite woody,
meaty, earthy, dark flavors; 25-year-old: sweet, caramel, toffee,
vanilla, tobacco, smoky, very smooth; "105": hot, spicy,
peppery, dry

GLENFIDDICH
Highland (Speyside)

The best-selling single malt whisky in the world, Glenfiddich is still owned and controlled by the family that founded it. The first malt was distilled in 1887. In the face of an uncomprehending whisky industry, Glenfiddich bottled, marketed, and sold its first single malt to a wide audience in 1963. Glenfiddich has an on-site cooperage, coal-fired stills, and its own bottling line. Glenfiddich is the only distillery in the Highland that distills, ages, and bottles in one location. It was also the first to construct a visitor center, which is one trip that should not be missed.

GLENFIDDICH DISTILLERY

Dufftown
Banffshire AB55 4DH / Scotland
Tel: +44 (0)1340 820373 / Fax: +44 (0)1340 820805
www.glenfiddich.com
Visitors' center: Yes

REGION: Highland (Speyside)

AGE WHEN BOTTLED: 12-year-old, 15-year-old Solera Reserve, 18-year-old Ancient Reserve, 30-year-old

STRENGTH: 12-year-old: 40%; 15-year-old: 40%; 18-year-old: 40%; 30-year-old: 43%

INDEPENDENT BOTTLINGS: Cadenhead

TASTING NOTES:

Aromas: Fruity and fresh
Flavors: Nutty, chocolate, sweet-spice

GLEN GARIOCH
Highland (Eastern)

One of the oldest distilleries in Scotland, Glen Garioch has records that go as far back as 1785. Well situated, with access to abundant sources of peat and fresh water, Glen Garioch also cleverly uses waste heat from the malting and distilling process to grow tomatoes in greenhouses on the property. Some of this whisky finds its way into Vat 69, as well as other blends.

GLEN GARIOCH DISTILLERY

Oldmeldrum
Inverurie
Aberdeenshire AB51 0ES / Scotland
Tel: +44 (0)1651 872706 / Fax: +44 (0)1651 872578
www.glengarioch.com
Visitors' center: No

REGION: Highland (Eastern)

AGE WHEN BOTTLED: 8-year-old, 15-year-old, 21-year-old

STRENGTH: 8-year-old: 40%; 15-year-old: 43%; 21-year-old: 43%

INDEPENDENT BOTTLINGS: Duncan Taylor & Co. (cask strength), Whisky Galore

TASTING NOTES:

  Aromas: Flowery and smoky, pleasant aromas
  Flavors: Peppery, with a hint of clove, some peat and smoke

GLENGOYNE
Highland (Southern)

Glengoygne is located directly on the imaginary line that divides the Highlands from the Lowlands. After being owned and operated for over one hundred years by the Lang family, the distillery was purchased in 1965 and completely modernized by Robertson & Baxter. The whisky is made by using malt and spring water that contain no peat. This whisky is probably the least peaty of all single malts. As it ages, however, it darkens in color and becomes more layered and complex on the nose and palate. A large amount is used for blending. Local legend has it that Rob Roy hid in a hollow tree near the distillery to avoid being captured.

GLENGOYNE DISTILLERY

Dumgoyne
Stirlingshire G63 9LB / Scotland
Tel: +44 (0)1360 550229 / Fax: +44 (0)1360 550094
www.glengoyne.com
Visitors' center: Yes

REGION: Highland (Southern)

AGE WHEN BOTTLED: 10-year-old, 17-year-old, 21-year-old, 30-year-old, Millennium (bottled 2000; no age declaration)

STRENGTH: 10-year-old: 40%; 17-year-old: 43%; 21-year-old: 43%; 30-year-old: 50%; Millennium: 50%

INDEPENDENT BOTTLINGS: None

TASTING NOTES:

Aromas: 10-year-old: very light, fresh, clean, a touch of mint and fruit; 17-year-old: floral, fruity, nutty

Flavors: 10-year-old: a bit sweet, light, citrus, a touch of pepper in the finish: 17-year-old: sweet, caramel, vanilla, woody on the finish

GLEN GRANT
HIGHLAND (SPEYSIDE)

Started in 1840, Glen Grant has been quite successful and, with the exception of a short period around the turn of the century, has continued to expand, producing whisky all year long. A large seller all over the world, it is very popular in Italy. Glen Grant casks that date back to the early 1950s have been independently bottled by Gordon & MacPhail. Tasting notes refer to 5-year-old.

GLEN GRANT DISTILLERY

Rothes
Morayshire AB38 7BS / Scotland
Tel: +44 (0)1542 783318 / Fax: +44 (0)1542 783306
Visitors' center: Yes

REGION: Highland (Speyside)

AGE WHEN BOTTLED: 5-year-old, 10-year-old, Glen Grant (no age declaration)

STRENGTH: 5-year-old: 40%; 10-year-old: 43%; Glen Grant: 40%

INDEPENDENT BOTTLINGS: Berry Brothers & Rudd, Cadenhead, Duncan Taylor & Co. (cask strength), Gordon & MacPhail, Hart Brothers, Scott's Selections, Signatory

TASTING NOTES:

Aromas: Light, fruity

Flavors: A touch sweet on the entry, very dry finish

PRODUCE OF SCOTLAND

GLENKEI

SINGLE HIGHLAND MALT
SCOTCH WHISKY

Distilled before
1983

750 ML.

A fragrant whisky
from the heart of
the Highlands.
GLEN KEITH
is prized by
experts for its
purity and depth
of flavour.

The pool of the Salmon

The Glen Keith distillery stands beside the fast-flowing ri
above a deep pool where wild salmon swim and leap. The Ga
linne a bhradan. Here, nature is unspoilt; the air and the wat
sweet. It is in the very heart of Scotch Whisky count

IMPORTED BY THE GLEN KEITH DISTILLING CO,
BOTTLED IN SCOTLAND

2GKF802

GLEN KEITH
Highland (Speyside)

The first new distillery in Scotland in the twentieth century, Glen Keith is also one of the most modern. The distillery uses gas-fired instead of coal-fired stills, and the whole operation is computerized. Mostly used for blending by Chivas Brothers, it is now available in a Seagram's bottling.

GLEN KEITH DISTILLERY

Keith
Banffshire AB55 3BU / Scotland
Tel: +44 (0)1542 783042 / Fax: +44 (0)1542 783056
Visitors' center: Yes

REGION: Highland (Speyside)

AGE WHEN BOTTLED: 10-year-old

STRENGTH: 43%

INDEPENDENT BOTTLINGS: Cadenhead, Duncan Taylor & Co. (cask strength), Gordon & MacPhail

TASTING NOTES:

  Aromas: Nutty, oily, a touch oaky
  Flavors: Soft, smooth, citrus, rich finish

GLENKINCHIE
LOWLAND

The entire production of Glenkinchie was used for blending until 1989, when a 10-year-old single malt bottling became available. This malt is a major component in the Haig family of blended whiskies, of which Haig and Haig Pinch are the most well-known in the United States. Glenkinchie is a dry, light, floral whisky exemplifying Lowland style. The distillery has a very interesting museum and visitors' center.

GLENKINCHIE DISTILLERY

Pentcaitland
East Lothian EH34 5ET / Scotland
Tel: +44 (0)1875 340333 / Fax: +44 (0)1875 340854
www.glenkinchie.com
Visitors' center: Yes

REGION: Lowland

AGE WHEN BOTTLED: 10-year-old

STRENGTH: 40%

INDEPENDENT BOTTLINGS: Cadenhead, Gordon & MacPhail

TASTING NOTES:

Aromas: Spicy, a bit hot, clean

Flavors: Medium weight, spicy, caramel, vanilla, dry mouth feel

Glenkinchie

THE EDINBURGH MALT
LOWLAND SCOTCH WHISKY

Glenkinchie Distillery was established in 1837 by John and George Rate. It is situated beside the Kinchie Burn in the heart of East Lothian farmland. Over the gently rolling hills around Glenkinchie, some of the finest barley is grown.

Glenkinchie Lowland Malt Whisky has a light delicate nose and a fresh clean aroma, the finish is smooth, with a subtle hint of dryness. A truly fine distinctive Single Malt, excellent as a pre-dinner drink.

10 YEARS OLD

43% alc/vol
DISTILLED AT THE GLENKINCHIE DISTILLERY
PENCAITLAND SCOTLAND
SOLE DISTRIBUTOR IN USA, SCHIEFFELIN & SOMERSET CO, NEW YORK, N.Y. PRODUCT OF SCOTLAND

750ml

THE GLENLIVET
HIGHLAND (SPEYSIDE)

Arguably the most famous single malt whisky in the world, the Glenlivet was the first licensed distillery in all of Scotland. This momentous event occurred in 1824. Due to the efficiency of the operation and the high quality of the product, the Glenlivet was being exported by the mid-1860s. Because the whisky's reputation for quality was so great, many other distilleries in and around the Livet Glen adopted the name Glenlivet. In the 1880s, the owners of the distillery filed suit and were awarded the sole ownership of the name *the* Glenlivet. A number of other distilleries in the region are allowed to use the name Glenlivet, but only as a hyphenated suffix, e.g., Longmorn-Glenlivet.

THE GLENLIVET DISTILLERY

Ballindalloch
Banffshire AB37 9DB / Scotland
Tel: +44 (0)1542 783220
www.glenlivet.com
Visitors' center: Yes

REGION: Highland (Speyside)

AGE WHEN BOTTLED: 12-year-old, 12-year-old "French Oak Finish," 12-year-old American Finish, 18-year-old, 21-year-old Archive, Cellar Collections vintages 1967, 1968, 1969, 1970, 1972

STRENGTH: All 12-year-olds: 40%; 18-year-old: 43%; 21-year-old: 43%; vintage bottlings range in strength

INDEPENDENT BOTTLINGS: Duncan Taylor & Co. (cask strength), Gordon & MacPhail, Hart Brothers, Murray McDavid, Signatory

TASTING NOTES:

Aromas: 12-year-old: oily, fruity, floral, slightly perfumed; 18-year-old: peaty, a touch hot, nutty, honey, vanilla

Flavors: 12-year-old: sweet, fruity, a bit smoky, caramel finish; 18-year-old: smoky, woody, coffee, tobacco, long layered finish, a touch spicy

GLENLOSSIE
HIGHLAND (SPEYSIDE)

Built in 1876, this distillery was taken over by Scottish Malt Distillers, Ltd., in 1919. It is now owned by United Distillers. The majority of the production goes for blending, and the distillery produces a 10-year-old bottling as well.

GLENLOSSIE DISTILLERY

Elgin
Morayshire IV30 3SS / Scotland
Tel: +44 (0)1343 860331 / Fax: +44 (0)1343 860302
Visitors' center: No

REGION: Highland (Speyside)

AGE WHEN BOTTLED: 10-year-old

STRENGTH: 43%

INDEPENDENT BOTTLINGS: Duncan Taylor & Co. (cask strength), Gordon & MacPhail, Hart Brothers, Signatory

TASTING NOTES:

Aromas: Perfumed and grassy

Flavors: Nutty and smooth with a little fruit

GLENMORANGIE
HIGHLAND (NORTHERN)

Legend has it that on the site of Glenmorangie, one form of alcoholic beverage or another has been produced since the Middle Ages. This distillery was also known for making various technical advances through innovative still design. A series of 12-year-old whiskies finished in different casks—Fino sherry, port, Cognac, Côte de Beaune, Sauternes, Madeira, rum, Malaga, Claret Wood, Burgundy Wood, and Tain l'Hermitage (Rhône wine barrel)—are marketed. Glenmorangie was the first to produce distillery-approved cask-strength bottlings and is also the largest selling malt in Scotland. Tasting notes refer to 18-year-old.

GLENMORANGIE DISTILLERY

Tain
Ross-shire IV19 1PZ / Scotland
Tel: +44 (0)1862 892043 / Fax: +44 (0)1862 893862
www.glenmorangie.com
Visitors' center: Yes

REGION: Highland (Northern)

AGE WHEN BOTTLED: 10-year-old; 18-year-old; wood finishes (no age declaration)

STRENGTH: 10-year-old: 40%; 18-year-old: 43%; wood finishes: 43%, except Côte de Beaune: 46%, rum: 45.9%, Madeira: 56.6%.

INDEPENDENT BOTTLINGS: None

TASTING NOTES:

Aromas: Nutty, floral hints, oily-tasting

Flavors: Smoky, coffee, tobacco, a touch of saltiness in the finish, full-flavored

GLEN MORAY
HIGHLAND (SPEYSIDE)

Originally a brewery, Glen Moray was turned into a distillery in 1897. Like its neighbor, Glenmorangie, Glen Moray offers a range of wood-finished malts. The distillery pioneered the use of white wine barrels for their wood-finish program.

GLEN MORAY DISTILLERY

Elgin
Morayshire IV30 1YE / Scotland
Tel: +44 (0)1343 542577 / Fax: +44 (0)1343 546195
www.glenmoray.com
Visitors' center: Yes

REGION: Highland (Speyside)

AGE WHEN BOTTLED: Single Speyside Malt (finished in Chardonnay barrel, no age declaration), 12-year-old (mellowed in Chenin Blanc), 16-year-old (mellowed in Chenin Blanc), 1981 Single Sherry Butt

STRENGTH: Single Speyside, 12-year-old, and 16-year-old: 40%; 1981: 57.7%

INDEPENDENT BOTTLINGS: Blackadder, Cadenhead

TASTING NOTES:

Aromas: Light, banana, grape

Flavors: Tropical, fruity, oak, resin finish

GLEN ORD
HIGHLAND (NORTHERN)

In the early nineteenth century, numerous illicit distilleries existed in the Northern Highlands of Scotland. The wave of localization starting in the 1820s sent many illegal distilleries on the straight and narrow. Many shuttered facilities were relicensed and transformed into new, legally approved production. Glen Ord, built on the site of an illicit distillery, was licensed in 1838. Using water to power some of the distillery operations-from its inception until the 1960s, Glen Ord is now quite a large, modern enterprise with its own malting facility. The distillery mixes in

heather with the peat to be used during the drying process, as the distillers believe this enhances the aromatics and flavors of the finished product. About 10 percent of the distillery output is bottled as single malt, the rest supplying blends such as Johnnie Walker and Dewar's. The malt has been bottled in the past under the names Glenordie, Ord, and Muir of Ord

GLEN ORD DISTILLERY

Muir of Ord
Ross-shire IV6 7UJ / Scotland
Tel: +44 (0)1463 870421 / Fax: +44 (0)1463 870101
www.glenord.com
Visitors' center: Yes

REGION: Highland (Northern)

AGE WHEN BOTTLED: 12-year-old

STRENGTH: 43%

INDEPENDENT BOTTLINGS: Cadenhead

TASTING NOTES:

Aromas: Nutty, grassy, a hint of floral
Flavors: Light, citrus, peach, very dry finish

GLEN ROTHES
Highland (Speyside)

Almost all of Glen Rothes is used for blending Famous Grouse and Cutty Sark. A large commercial concern, this distillery produces over 1 million gallons of whisky annually. The firm of Berry Brothers & Rudd has chosen Glen Rothes to be their house single malt whisky. Berry Brothers is also responsible for the famous blended whisky Cutty Sark, of which Glen Rothes is a component. The Glen Rothes single malt bottlings have both date of distillation and date of bottling on the label.

GLEN ROTHES DISTILLERY

Rothes
Morayshire AB38 7AA / Scotland
Tel: +44 (0)1340 831248 / Fax: +44 (0)1340 831484
www.glenrothewhisky.com
Visitors' center: No

REGION: Highland (Speyside)

AGE WHEN BOTTLED: 1989, 1973

STRENGTH: 1989: 43%; 1973: 43%

INDEPENDENT BOTTLINGS: Cadenhead, Duncan Taylor & Co., Gordon & MacPhail, Master of Malt, Signatory, Whisky Galore

TASTING NOTES:

Aromas: Complex, spicy, light peat, nutty

Flavors: Caramel, buttery, vanilla, sweet, smoky finish

GLEN SCOTIA
CAMPBELTOWN

In the nineteenth century, Campbeltown possessed the greatest concentration of distilleries in all of Scotland; now only two still produce whisky. Because the town's distilleries sold lots of mediocre whisky for a long time, the name Campbeltown became associated with producing a less than quality product. Now the region of Campbeltown is producing high-quality malt; Glen Scotia is in good company with Springbank, the other operating Campbeltown distillery. Opened and closed a number of times during the past one hundred years, Glen Scotia last closed in 1994. It was bought in 1999 by the Loch Lomond Company and is now in production. The distillery is rumored to be haunted.

GLEN SCOTIA

12 High Street
Campbeltown
Argyllshire PA28 6DS / Scotland
Tel: +44 (0) 1586 552 288
Visitors' center: No

REGION: Campbeltown

AGE WHEN BOTTLED: 12-year-old, 14-year-old, 17-year-old

STRENGTH: 12-, 14-, and 17-year-old: all 43%

INDEPENDENT BOTTLINGS: Cadenhead, Signatory

TASTING NOTES:

  Aromas: Sweet, fruity, floral
  Flavors: Heavy, oily, peaty, fat

GLENTAUCHERS
HIGHLAND (SPEYSIDE)

This distillery produces very few bottlings. It was rebuilt in 1965, closed in 1985, and reopened in 1989. It's used as a main component in Black & White.

GLENTAUCHERS DISTILLERY

Mulben
Keith
Banffshire AB55 6YL / Scotland
Tel: +44 (0)1542 860272 / Fax: +44 (0)1542 860327
Visitors' center: No

REGION: Highland (Speyside)

AGE WHEN BOTTLED: 15-year-old

STRENGTH: 46%

INDEPENDENT BOTTLINGS: Cadenhead, Duncan Taylor & Co. cask strength, Gordon & MacPhail, Signatory

TASTING NOTES:

    Aromas: Volatile, sharp

    Flavors: Dried fruit, hot

THE TOP FIVE MARKETS FOR SCOTCH BY VOLUME ARE
1. FRANCE
2. UNITED KINGDOM
3. SPAIN
4. UNITED STATES
5. SOUTH KOREA

GLENTURRET
HIGHLAND (SOUTHERN)

There is evidence that illicit distilling took place here as far back as 1717. Competition continues between Glenturret and Edradour over the claim of which is the smallest distillery in Scotland. Glenturret, established in 1775, was bought in 1959, and under the skilled guidance of James Fairlie has produced numerous award-winning whiskies through the years. In 1981, Glenturret was bought by French liqueur makers, Cointreau SA, and then taken over in 1990 by Highland Distilleries, now called the Edrington Group. The distillery possesses a very sophisticated visitors' center and a statue of its late, record-breaking cat, Towser. Lots of distilleries keep cats handy because mice like to eat grain. In Towser's lifetime he was reputed to have dispatched 28,899 mice.

GLENTURRET DISTILLERY

Crieff
Perthshire PH7 4HA / Scotland
Tel: +44 (0)1764 656565 / Fax: +44 (0)1764 654366
Visitors' center: Yes

REGION: Highland (Southern)

AGE WHEN BOTTLED: 12-year-old

STRENGTH: 12-year-old: 40%; 15-year-old: 50%; 18-year-old: 40%

INDEPENDENT BOTTLINGS: Gordon & MacPhail, Murray McDavid, Signatory

TASTING NOTES:

Aromas: Peaty, grassy, and full-bodied

Flavors: Creamy and zesty

HIGHLAND PARK
ISLAND (ORKNEY)

Highland Park, the most northerly distillery in Scotland, sits on what was originally the site of an illicit still run by Magnus Eunson. Mr. Eunson was also the local preacher and managed to evade tax officials by hiding his whisky in a number of creative locations. According to some, this distillery was clandestinely operating since the 1790s but then became licensed as a legitimate business in 1824. The peat used for malting the barley is locally grown and mixed with heather, which is said to add a distinctive note to the whisky. This very highly rated malt is one of the world's best sellers. Tasting notes refer to 12-year-old.

HIGHLAND PARK DISTILLERY

Kirkwall
Orkney, KW15 1SU / Scotland
Tel: +44 (0)1856 873107 / Fax: +44 (0)1856 876091
www.highlandpark.co.uk
Visitors' center: Yes

REGION: Island (Orkney)

AGE WHEN BOTTLED: 15-year-old, 18-year-old, 25-year-old

STRENGTH: 12-year-old: 40%; 15-year-old: 40%; 18-year-old: 43%; 25-year-old: 50.7%

INDEPENDENT BOTTLINGS: Adelphi, Cadenhead, Duncan Taylor & Co. (cask strength), Gordon & MacPhail, Hart Brothers, Murray McDavid, Signatory, Whisky Galore

TASTING NOTES:

  Aromas: Nutty, faintly oily, peaty

  Flavors: Smoky, caramel, fruity peach and citrus, a hint of salt, long finish

IMPERIAL
HIGHLAND (SPEYSIDE)

Imperial was part of a group consisting of Dailuaine and Talisker. This distillery has closed and reopened several times over the course of the last century. Since 1998, it has been out of production. Several years ago a 15-year-old bottling from the distillery was released.

IMPERIAL DISTILLERY

Carron by Aberlour
Banffshire AB43 9QP / Scotland
Tel: +44 (0)1340 810276 / Fax: +44 (0)1340 810563
Visitors' center: By appointment only

REGION: Highland (Speyside)

AGE WHEN BOTTLED: 15-year-old

STRENGTH: 46%

INDEPENDENT BOTTLINGS: Cadenhead, Gordon & MacPhail, Signatory

TASTING NOTES:

Aromas: Spicy, a little nutty
Flavors: Slight touch of vanilla

INCHGOWER
Highland (Speyside)

The Tochineal Distillery, built in 1824 and located at the mouth of the Spey River, was originally the site of what is now Inchgower. The distillery was moved in 1936 to a spot nearer the coast, in search of larger quarters and a more reliable water source. Inchgower was acquired by Arthur Bell & Sons, which subsequently became a part of United Distillers.

INCHGOWER DISTILLERY

Buckie
Banffshire AB56 2AB / Scotland
Tel: +44 (0)1542 831161 / Fax: +44 (0)1542 834531
Visitors' center: No

REGION: Highlands (Speyside)

AGE WHEN BOTTLED: 14-year-old

STRENGTH: 43%

INDEPENDENT BOTTLINGS: Master of Malt, Oddbins, Whisky Galore

TASTING NOTES:

  Aromas: Rich, vanilla, hint of saline
  Flavors: Buttery and sweet, dry finish

ISLE OF JURA
ISLAND (JURA)

Jura means "deer" in Norse. There is evidence that distilling has taken place on this island since the 1600s. George Orwell wrote *1984* on wild and remote Jura Island. In his honor, a bottling called Orwell is produced. Very tall stills are employed so that only the lightest alcohol goes over the top, creating a lighter whisky. The distillery's 36-year-old single malt Special Collector's Edition won Gold World Medal at the 2002 New York Festivals Awards.

ISLE OF JURA DISTILLERY

Jura
Argyllshire PA60 7XT / Scotland
Tel: +44 (0)1496 820240 / Fax: +44 (0)1496 820344
www.isleofjura.com
Visitors' center: Yes

REGION: Island (Jura)

AGE WHEN BOTTLED: Superstion: no age declaration; 10-year-old, 16-year-old, 21-year-old, 27-year-old, 33-year-old, 36-year-old

STRENGTH: Superstion: 43%; 10-year-old: 40%; 16-year-old: 40%; 21-year-old: 43%; 27-year-old: 45%; 33-year-old: 55.6%; 36-year-old: 63.7%.

INDEPENDENT BOTTLINGS: Adelphi, Gordon & MacPhail, Signatory

TASTING NOTES:

   Aromas: Minty, smoky, grassy
   Flavors: Dry, salty, peppery

KNOCKANDO
HIGHLAND (SPEYSIDE)

This distillery reopened in 1904 and was acquired in 1952 by the producers of J & B. Much of the whisky is used in blending, but the distillery has a fairly large capacity, so it is easily found in retail shops. The whisky is bottled not according to a specific calendar, but when the distillery manager feels it is at its peak. The bottle bears both the date of distillation and the date of bottling. Extra Old Reserve 21-year-old is also available, although sometimes it turns out to be even a little older than twenty-one years.

KNOCKANDO DISTILLERY

Knockando
Morayshire AB38 7RT / Scotland
Tel: +44 (0)1340 810205 / Fax: +44 (0)1340 810369
www.malts.com
Visitors' center: Yes

REGION: Highland (Speyside)

AGE WHEN BOTTLED: 12-year-old, 15-year-old, 18-year-old, 21-year-old

STRENGTH: 12-year-old: 40%; 15-year-old: 40%; 18-year-old: 43%; 21-year-old: 43%

INDEPENDENT BOTTLINGS: Duncan Taylor & Co. (cask strength), Signatory

TASTING NOTES:

  Aromas: Spicy, nutty, and a bit hot on the nose
  Flavors: Light, peppery, clean finish

LAGAVULIN
ISLAY

Claim is made that distilling has taken place on this site as far back as 1742. The distillery now known as Lagavulin was built during the early part of the last century, probably in the 1820s. The majority of this whisky is used for blending. In its early days, most of Lagavulin's production was used as the base for White Horse blended whisky. The water used in the production of the whisky has high peat content, and the storage warehouse for the casks is right on the sea. Both aspects contribute to the intensity of flavor in this malt.

LAGAVULIN DISTILLERY

Port Ellen
Isle of Islay
Argyll PA42 7DZ / Scotland
Tel: +44 (0)1496 302400 / Fax: +44 (0)1496 202733
www.malts.com
Visitors' center: Yes

REGION: Islay

AGE WHEN BOTTLED: 16-year-old

STRENGTH: 43%

INDEPENDENT BOTTLINGS: Cadenhead, Murray McDavid

TASTING NOTES:

  Aromas: Peat, iodine, floral

  Flavors: Smoky, very peaty, salty, full-bodied

BY APPOINTMENT TO
HER MAJESTY THE QUEEN
SCOTCH WHISKY DISTILLERS
WHITE HORSE DISTILLERS LTD. GLASGOW.

LAGAVULIN
DISTILLERY
ESTᴰ 1816 ISLᴀ
REGISTERED
Mackie & Co

LAGAVULIN

SINGLE ISLAY MALT WHISKY

AGED **16** YEARS

SCOTCH WHISKY

...water, passing over rocky falls, steeped in mountain air and ...land peat, distilled and matured in oak casks exposed to the sea ...her Lagavulin's robust and smoky character. Time, say the Islanders, ...TAKES OUT THE FIRE but LEAVES IN THE WARMTH ...E HORSE OF SUINABHAL" – By William Black. – "I hel... ...interest myself, and I hef been close to the 'Lagavulin 'Distille... ...the spring that will make the 'Lagavulin 'Whisky just as fine... ...White Horse Distillers, Gl...

Years 10 Old
BOTTLED IN SCOTLAND
LAPHROAIG®
SINGLE ISLAY MALT
SCOTCH WHISKY
10
Years Old
The most richly flavoured of
all Scotch whiskies
ESTABLISHED
1815
DISTILLED AND BOTTLED IN SCOTLAND BY
D. JOHNSTON & CO., (LAPHROAIG), LAPHROAIG DISTILLERY, ISLE OF ISLAY.
PRODUCT OF SCOTLAND
750ml
43% alc/vol

LAPHROAIG
HIGHLAND (NORTHERN)

Built around 1820, this distillery produces a very individual whisky. Popular wisdom has it that close proximity to the coast contributes a distinctly briny or saline quality to the whisky. Many producers hold that the exchange of salt air and whisky in barrel creates this unique flavor. Laphroaig's producers believe that it is the high content of moss in the peat used during the malting process that gives the whisky its unique flavor. Another nice note that adds "flavor" to the character of this distillery is that in 1954 the owner left the distillery to Bessie Williamson, his assistant. She ran the company quite successfully until she retired in 1972.

LAPHROAIG DISTILLERY

Port Ellen
Isle of Islay
Argyllshire PA42 7DU / Scotland
Tel: +44 (0)1496 302418 / Fax: +44 (0)1496 302496
www.laphroaig.com
Visitors' center: Yes

REGION: Highland (Northern)

AGE WHEN BOTTLED: 10-year-old, 15-year-old, 30-year-old (bottled 1997), 40-year-old

STRENGTH: 10-year-old: 40%; 15-year-old: 43%; 30-year-old: 43%; 40-year-old: 42.3%

INDEPENDENT BOTTLINGS: Cadenhead, Murray McDavid, Signatory

TASTING NOTES:

Aromas: 10-year-old: peaty, smoky, medicinal; 15-year-old: medicinal, peaty, citrus

Flavors: 10-year-old: iodine, smoky, quite intense saltiness, finishes sharply; 15-year-old: a touch sweet, peppery, smoky, long sweet, sour finish

LINKWOOD
HIGHLAND (SPEYSIDE)

Built around 1821, Linkwood was expanded in the late 1860s. Rumor has it that one of the still masters was so convinced that any change in the still house would affect the whiskey's character that he refused to have even a spider's web removed. Almost all of the distillery's production goes for blending.

LINKWOOD DISTILLERY

Elgin
Morayshire IV30 3RD / Scotland
Tel: +44 (0)1343 547004 / Fax: +44 (0)1343 549449
Visitors' center: By appointment only

REGION: Highland (Speyside)

AGE WHEN BOTTLED: 12-year-old

STRENGTH: 43%

INDEPENDENT BOTTLINGS: Cadenhead, Duncan Taylor & Co. (cask strength), Gordon & MacPhail, Hart Brothers, Signatory

TASTING NOTES:

Aromas: Sweet, faintly peaty aromas

Flavors: Caramel, sweetish, very clean

AGED **8** YEARS

PRODUCT OF SCOTLAND

LITTLEMILL ®

Established
1772

SINGLE LOWLAND MALT
SCOTCH WHISKY

DISTILLED AND BOTTLED IN SCOTLAND BY
LITTLEMILL DISTILLERY CO. LTD.
BOWLING, DUNBARTONSHIRE, SCOTLAND

43% Alc./Vol.
(86 Proof)

Imported by
JOHN GROSS & CO.
Baltimore, MD.

750ml

LITTLEMILL

LOWLAND

This is possibly Scotland's oldest Lowland distillery. It appears that some form of brewing and then distilling has been performed on this site since the fourteenth century. Classified as a Lowland distillery, Littlemill uses water and peat from Highland sources. Most of the whisky produced is used in blending, but the distillery bottled some single malt, which is still available. Littlemill is now closed.

LITTLEMILL DISTILLERY

Bowling
Dumbartonshire G60 5BG / Scotland
Tel: +44 (0)1389 752781
Visitors' center: No

REGION: Lowland

AGE WHEN BOTTLED: 8-year-old

STRENGTH: 43%

INDEPENDENT BOTTLINGS: Cadenhead, Ian McLeod, Signatory

TASTING NOTES:

   Aromas: Spicy, hot, a touch nutty

   Flavors: Sweet, vanilla, caramel, peachy, a bit peppery on the finish

LOCH LOMOND
(INCHMURRIN & OLD RHOSDHU)
HIGHLAND (SOUTHERN)

Built on the site of an old printing plant, Loch Lomond became operational in 1966. The distillery sits right on top of the imaginary line that divides Highland from Lowland. The stills used at Loch Lomond are designed to distill different weights of whisky. In addition to producing Inchmurrin, the distillery also produces a stronger whisky called Rhosdhu. Tasting notes refer to Inchmurrin.

LOCH LOMOND DISTILLERY

Alexandria
Dumbertonshire G83 0TL / Scotland
Tel: +44 (0)1389 752781 / Fax: +44 (0)1389 757977
www.lochlomonddistillery.com
Visitors' center: No

REGION: Highland (Southern)

AGE WHEN BOTTLED: Inchmurren: 10-year-old; Loch Lomond: no age declaration; Old Rhosdhu: no age declaration

STRENGTH: Inchmurren, Loch Lomond, and Old Rhosdhu: all 40%

INDEPENDENT BOTTLINGS: Cadenhead, Gordon & MacPhail

TASTING NOTES:

Aromas: Rubbery, nutty, cheesy nose

Flavors: Hot, a bit green, woody, strong, unbalanced character

LONGMORN
Highland (Speyside)

Longmorn distillery began operations in 1897, and along with Glen Grant, was acquired by the Glenlivet distilleries in 1970. A corruption from the Gaelic, *longmorn* means "the place of the holy man." The distillery was built on a site that was thought previously to house an ancient chapel.

LONGMORN DISTILLERY

Elgin
Morayshire IV30 3SJ / Scotland
Tel: +44 (0)1542 783400 / Fax: +44 (0)1542 783404
Visitors' center: By appointment only

REGION: Highland (Speyside)

AGE WHEN BOTTLED: 12-year-old, 15-year-old

STRENGTH: 12-year-old: 40%; 15-year-old: 45%

INDEPENDENT BOTTLINGS: Blackadder, Duncan Taylor & Co. (cask strength), Gordon & MacPhail, Hart Brothers, Scott's Selection, Signatory, Whisky Galore

TASTING NOTES:

Aromas: Caramel, fruity
Flavors: Weighty, fresh, sweetish-peppery finish

THE MACALLAN
HIGHLAND (SPEYSIDE)

The Macallan was officially licensed to operate and pay taxes in 1824 (a few months after the Glenlivet became legal). It was founded on a site, surely used for illicit distilling, in a great, secluded location with access to abundant sources of peat, barley, and fresh water. The distillery was bought by Roderick Kemp, a larger-than-life figure in the history of the whisky business. His descendants are still involved in the firm's operation. Some of the distinctive features of this distillery are its use of small, squat, copper pot stills, whose shape is said to contribute to a creamy style of whisky. Also, its sherry-seasoned barrels set the Macallan apart; other distillers use bourbon-, port-, or Madeira-flavored barrels. In 1976, Macallan started to buy its own oak, dry it, make the barrels, and season them in Jerez at various sherry bodegas, rather than continuing to reuse sherry barrels used for export from Jerez. After three to four years, the casks are deemed ready and shipped to the distillery. Approximately 70 percent of the malt is matured in first-fill casks, the rest in second-fill casks.

In the spring of 1997, two monumental events occurred: a bottle of 1874 Macallan was discovered in the hold of a sunken ship and sold at auction (back to the distillery), and the distillery was purchased by Highland-Suntory. In the case of the former event, a replica of the 1874 was produced. The whiskies contained therein were blended from 18- to 26-year-old malt matured in sherry casks. As regards the latter, after just two years, Highland-Suntory was acquired by the Edrington Group. The new owners have declared that they have no intention of changing anything about the Macallan.

THE MACALLAN DISTILLERY

Craigellachie
Banffshire AB38 9RX / Scotland
Tel: +44 (0)1340 871471 / Fax: +44 (0)1340 871212
www.macallan.com
Visitors' center: Yes

REGION: Highland (Speyside)

AGE WHEN BOTTLED: 12-year-old, 18-year-old, 25-year-old, 30-year-old, 18-year-old "Gran Reserva" (matured in first-fill sherry cask); 12-year-old cask strength: no age declaration; Vintage (1945–1972, bottled in 2002)

STRENGTH: 12-, 18-, 25-, and 30-year-old: all 43%; Gran Reserva: 40%; cask strength: 58.6%; Vintages range in strength

INDEPENDENT BOTTLINGS: Adelphi, Cadenhead, Duncan Taylor & Co. (cask strength), Gordon & MacPhail, Murray McDavid, Signatory, Whisky Galore

TASTING NOTES:

Aromas: 12-year-old: fruity, sherried, vanilla; 18-year-old: caramel, toffee, hint of smoke, nutty.

Flavors: 12-year-old: citrus, a touch salty, hint of smoke, long, slightly oily finish; 18-year-old: very smooth, complex, vanilla, caramel, tobacco, nutty, long very layered finish. Heavy, rich chocolate, orange, molasses, long dark finish.

MANNOCHMORE
SPEYSIDE

Built by John Haig & Co. in 1971 to contribute to Haig's blends, the distillery was mothballed in 1985 and reopened in 1989. In addition to making Mannochmore, the distillery produces Loch Dhu, "the Black Whisky." Tasting notes refer to the Loch Dhu.

MANNOCHMORE DISTILLERY

Elgin
Morayshire IV30 3SS / Scotland
Tel: +44 (0)1343 860331 / Fax: +44 (0)1343 860302
www.malts.com
Visitors' center: No

REGION: Speyside

AGE WHEN BOTTLED: 12-year-old, 22-year-old (distilled 1974, bottled 1997), 10-year-old Loch Dhu

STRENGTH: 12-year-old: 43%; 22-year-old: 60.1%; 10-year-old Loch Dhu: 40%

INDEPENDENT BOTTLINGS: Cadenhead, Chieftain's Choice, Cooper's Choice, Gordon & MacPhail, Scott's Selection

TASTING NOTES:

   Aromas: Hot, banana, mint
   Flavors: Burnt, anise, sweet

MILTONDUFF
Highland (Speyside)

Established in 1824 by Andrew Peary and Robert Bain on the former site of a priory, the distillery was purchased in 1866 by William Stuart. In the 1890s, Thomas Yool & Co. joined Stuart and extended the distillery. In 1936 it was taken over by Hiram Walker-Gooderham & Worts Ltd. Hiram Walker and Sons (Scotland) Ltd. took control the following year. It was rebuilt in 1974. In 1992, Allied Distillers took over. The majority of its production is used in Ballantine's blends. From the early 1960s until 1981, another malt called Mosstowie was produced at Miltonduff. Some independent bottlings of Mosstowie may still be found.

MILTONDUFF DISTILLERY

Elgin
Morayshire IV30 3TQ / Scotland
Tel: +44 (0)1343 547433 / Fax: +44 (0)1343 548802
Visitors' center: Yes

REGION: Highland (Speyside)

AGE WHEN BOTTLED: 12-year-old

STRENGTH: 40%

INDEPENDENT BOTTLINGS: Blackadder International (Mosstowie), Cadenhead, Duncan Taylor & Co. (cask strength), Gordon & MacPhail, Hart Brothers, Signatory

TASTING NOTES:

Aromas: Light, fresh, floral notes
Flavors: Herbal, slightly sweet, bright finish

MORTLACH
HIGHLAND (SPEYSIDE)

In Gaelic, *mortlach* means "bowl-shaped valley." The brand name now stands as a quaint reminder of the inextricable relationship between Scotch whisky and geography. Mortlach is used as a major component in several blends, including Johnnie Walker Red Label. A large distillery, initially modernized in 1903, Mortlach has operated continuously since 1823, except for a brief interruption during World War II. Tasting notes refer to 15-year-old Gordon & MacPhail bottling.

MORTLACH DISTILLERY

Dufftown
Keith
Banffshire AB55 4AQ / Scotland
Tel: +44 (0)1340 820318 / Fax: +44 (0)1340 820019
Visitors' center: No

REGION: Highland (Speyside)

AGE WHEN BOTTLED: 16-year-old, 22-year-old (distilled 1972)

STRENGTH: 16-year-old: 43%; 22-year-old: 65.3%

INDEPENDENT BOTTLINGS: Adelphi, Blackadder International, Cadenhead, Duncan Taylor & Co. (cask strength), Gordon & MacPhail, Hart Brothers, Whisky Galore

TASTING NOTES:

Aromas: Light, fresh, fruity

Flavors: Smoky, woody, hints of vanilla, caramel; more layered than nose would indicate

0ml 40%alc/v (80Prod

YEARS **15** OLD

Mortlach

Rare Old *Highland Malt*

SCOTCH WHISKY

Proprietors
GEORGE COWIE & SON LTD
MORTLACH GLENLIVET DISTILLERY DUFFTOWN

Matured & Bottled by
GORDON & MACPHAIL
ELGIN SCOTLAND

UNBLENDED   POT STILL

NORTH PORT
HIGHLAND (EASTERN)

North Port was founded in the 1820s by a local farmer. It was named after the north gate in the walls that surrounded the city in ancient times. North Port closed in 1983 and has since been demolished. A few independent bottlings may still be found.

REGION: Highland (Eastern)

AGE WHEN BOTTLED: NA

STRENGTH: NA

TASTING NOTES:

Aromas: NA

Flavors: NA

OBAN
HIGHLAND (WESTERN)

Oban Distillery is situated in the center of town overlooking the sea. This small fishing village was first inhabited in BC 5000. Celts and Vikings have also lived there. Some important very early archeological remains were found on the site of the distillery. Much of Oban's output goes for blending, but, over time, Oban has established a devoted following.

OBAN DISTILLERY

Oban
Argyll PA34 5NH / Scotland
Tel: +44 (0)1631 562110 / Fax: +44 (0)1631 563344
www.malts.com
Visitors' center: Yes

REGION: Highland (Western)

AGE WHEN BOTTLED: 14-year-old, 1980 "Double Matured" finished in Fino wood

STRENGTH: 14-year-old: 43%; 1980: 43%

INDEPENDENT BOTTLINGS: Cadenhead, Gordon & MacPhail

TASTING NOTES:

Aromas: Nutty, smoky, spicy

Flavors: Smoky and smooth

OLD PULTENEY
HIGHLAND (SPEYSIDE)

James Henderson founded Pulteney in 1826, and it subsequently closed from 1926 to 1951. Purchased in 1955 by Hiram Walker, Pulteney is used almost exclusively for blending; 1997 saw the release of an "official" 12-year-old bottling.

PULTENEY DISTILLERY

Huddart Street
Wick
Caithness KW1 5BA / Scotland
Tel: +44 (0)1955 602371 / Fax: +44 (0)1955 602279
www.oldpulteney.com
Visitors' center: Yes

REGION: Highland (Speyside)

AGE WHEN BOTTLED: 12-year-old, 18-year-old

STRENGTH: 12-year-old: 40%; 18-year-old: 59.1%

INDEPENDENT BOTTLINGS: Duncan Taylor & Co. (cask strength), Gordon & MacPhail (Connoisseurs Choice), Signatory, Whisky Galore

TASTING NOTES:

   Aromas: Slight spice and sweet nose
   Flavors: Peaty and slightly smoky

PORT ELLEN
ISLAY

Established in 1825, this distillery was silent from 1929 to 1966. Major renovations were made in 1967, instituting the use of four stills. The maltings continue to supply many Islay distilleries, but Port Ellen stopped production in 1983. Some independent bottlings may be found. Tasting notes refer to a 1980 "Connoisseurs Choice" Gordon & MacPhail bottling.

PORT ELLEN DISTILLERY

Port Ellen
Isle of Islay
Argyllshire PA42 7AH / Scotland
Visitors' center: No

REGION: Islay

AGE WHEN BOTTLED: 1980 Vintage

STRENGTH: 40%

INDEPENDENT BOTTLINGS: Douglas Laing, Gordon & MacPhail, Signatory

TASTING NOTES:

  Aromas: Peaty, smoky, and petroly
  Flavors: Oaky, buttery, and smoky

ROSEBANK
LOWLAND

James Rankine established Rosebank on the site of the prior Camelon distillery in 1840. It was rebuilt by his son in 1864. Rosebank's process involved triple-distilling with one wash still and two spirit stills. The distillery enjoyed a fine reputation for many years, and in 1914 the Rosebank Distillery was one of the founders of Scottish Malt Distillers—now part of United Distillers. Rosebank closed in May 1993. In 2003, a 12-year-old was released from the last of the stocks.

ROSEBANK DISTILLERY

Falkirk
Stirlingshire FK1 5BW / Scotland
Visitors' center: No

REGION: Lowland

AGE WHEN BOTTLED: 12-year-old

STRENGTH: 43%

TASTING NOTES:

Aromas: Petrol and grass tones
Flavors: Peaty and full-bodied

ROYAL BRACKLA

Highland (Northern)

Use of the prefix "Royal" was granted to this whisky in a show of approval by King William IV in 1835. In 1898, Brackla Distillery Company was formed and more land not far from Cawdor Castle was acquired for expansion, from the Earl of Cawdor. After a few changes of hands, the distillery was modernized in 1965 when steam-fired stills with a capacity of 5,000 gallons each were added.

ROYAL BRACKLA DISTILLERY

Cawdor
Nairn
Nairnshire IV12 5QY / Scotland
Tel: +44 (0)1667 404280 / Fax: +44 (0)1667 404743
Visitors' center: No

REGION: Highland (Northern)

AGE WHEN BOTTLED: 10-year-old

STRENGTH: 43%

INDEPENDENT BOTTLINGS: Blackadder International, Douglas Laing & Co., Gordon & MacPhail, Hart Brothers, Murray McDavid, Scott's Selections

TASTING NOTES:

  Aromas: Clean, fruity, and peaty
  Flavors: A sweet, yet well-balanced fullness

AGED 12 YEARS
SINGLE MALT

ROYAL
LOCHNAGAR
Single Highland Malt
SCOTCH WHISKY
Produced in Scotland
BY
Royal Lochnagar Distillery

CRATHIE, DEESIDE
ABERDEENSHIRE
SCOTLAND

750ml   40% Alc/Vol

EST? 1845

BY APPOINTMENT TO THEIR LATE MAJESTIES
QUEEN VICTORIA, KING EDWARD VII & KING GEORGE V

R
LOC
SELECT
Single H
SCOTC
Produ
Royal Loc

750ml

EST

The diary of John B

"I asked Prince A...
H.R.H. having agreed
(which had been prev...
glace to Her Majesty, S
the Prince, I then pres...
to the Prince of Wales..."

As a result of thi...
privilege of calling its
be accorded this hono...
the spirit."

ROYAL LOCHNAGAR
HIGHLAND (EASTERN)

Lochnagar became the distillery to the royal household at the time of Queen Victoria, hence the name "Royal." The phrase "take a peg of John Begg" was an early advertising slogan used by Royal Lochnager, as this distillery was built by John Begg in 1845. Much of this whisky is used in blending. Various individual casks of different ages are bottled occasionally and sold as Royal Lochnagar Selected Reserve.

ROYAL LOCHNAGAR DISTILLERY

Ballater
Aberdeenshire AB35 5TB / Scotland
Tel: +44 (0)1339 742273 / Fax: +44 (0)1339 742312
www.malts.com
Visitors' center: Yes

REGION: Highland (Eastern)

AGE WHEN BOTTLED: 12-year-old, Selected Reserve (no age declaration)

STRENGTH: 12-year-old: 40%; Selected Reserve: 43%

INDEPENDENT BOTTLINGS: Hart Brothers

TASTING NOTES:

  Aromas: Floral, fruity, good aromatics

  Flavors: Pepper, hint of vanilla, woody, very persistent, lingering finish

SCAPA
ISLAND (ORKNEY)

Located on the very beautiful—if you like remote—island of Orkney, this distillery opened in 1885 and produced whisky until 1994. A 10-year-old and a 12-year-old are available, as well as many independent bottlings.

SCAPA DISTILLERY

St. Ola
Orkney KW15 1SE / Scotland
Tel: +44 (0)1856 872071 / Fax: +44 (0)1856 876585
Visitors' center: No

REGION: Island (Orkney)

AGE WHEN BOTTLED: 10-year-old, 12-year-old

STRENGTH: 10-year-old: 43%; 12-year-old: 40%

INDEPENDENT BOTTLINGS: Blackadder International, Cadenhead, Douglas Laing, Gordon & MacPhail, Signatory, SMWS

TASTING NOTES:

Aromas: Oily nose, a bit of fruit and vanilla

Flavors: Some caramel and vanilla, oily finish

SPEYBURN
HIGHLAND (SPEYSIDE)

Known as the "Gibbet," because of its location near the ancient Cnock na Croiche, or Hillock of the Gibbet, the distillery was built in 1897 by John Hopkins & Co. Although it continued to use a horse and cart into the 1950s (when it finally got a tractor), it was the first Scottish malt distillery to install a steam-driven mechanical malting system.

SPEYBURN DISTILLERY

Rothes
Aberlour
Morayshire AB38 7AG / Scotland
Tel: +44 (0)1340 831213 / Fax: +44 (0)1340 831678
www.speyburndistillery.com
Visitors' center: No

REGION: Highland (Speyside)

AGE WHEN BOTTLED: 10-year-old, 21-year-old Single Cask 1979

STRENGTH: 10-year-old: 40%; 21-year-old: 60.1%

INDEPENDENT BOTTLINGS: Gordon & MacPhail

TASTING NOTES:

  Aromas: Fresh, floral
  Flavors: Light, spicy

THE TOP FIVE SCOTCH MARKETS BY DOLLAR VOLUME ARE
1. UNITED STATES
2. SPAIN
3. FRANCE
4. SOUTH KOREA
5. JAPAN

SPEYSIDE
HIGHLAND

In 1962, George Christie built this distillery in the centuries-old "dry stane dyking" method, that is, stone structures put together without any mortar, opposite the former Drumguish distillery. It took him thirty years to complete, and the first distillation took place in 1990. See also Drumguish, page 98.

SPEYSIDE DISTILLERY

Glen Tromie
Kingussie
Inverness-shire PH21 1NS / Scotland
Tel: +44 (0)1540 661060 / Fax: +44 (0)1540 661959
www.speyside.com
Visitors' center: No

REGION: Highland

AGE WHEN BOTTLED: 12-year-old

STRENGTH: 43%

INDEPENDENT BOTTLINGS: Scott's Selection

TASTING NOTES:

   Aromas: Lightly smoky, oily
   Flavors: Caramel, vanilla

SPRINGBANK
CAMPBELTOWN

Springbank has been owned by the same family since 1935. They are the direct descendents of the founding Mitchell family whose ownership dates back to 1837. The distillery does not chill-filter or add artificial color to its whisky and uses its own malt exclusively. In addition, Springbank possesses its own bottling line so that the distillery can produce, mature, and bottle all on the same premises. Equipped to triple-distill, the Springbank bottlings are "two and one half times" distilled. Longrow, a label resurrected by the distillery, is double-distilled and has lots of peat character. Another revived label, Hazelburn, is made from unpeated malt and triple-distilled. Campbeltown, once a center of whisky distilling, has gone from having thirty functioning distilleries to now having only two. Springbank has played a major role in the resurgence of this once-esteemed whisky region.

SPRINGBANK DISTILLERY

Campbeltown
Argyll PA28 6EJ / Scotland
Tel: +44 (0)1586 552085 / Fax: +44 (0)1586 553215
www.springbankdistillers.com
Visitors' center: By appointment only

REGION: Campbeltown

AGE WHEN BOTTLED: 10-year-old, 12-year-old, 15-year-old, 25-year-old, Longrow 10-year-old

STRENGTH: 10-, 15-, and 25-year-old, and Longrow 10-year-old: all 46%

INDEPENDENT BOTTLINGS: Adelphi, Blackadder, Duncan Taylor & Co. (cask strength), Hart Brothers, Murray McDavid, Signatory, Whisky Galore

TASTING NOTES:

Aromas: Briny, peppery, vanilla

Flavors: Layered; sweet, salty, spicy, long finish

STRATHISLA
HIGHLAND (SPEYSIDE)

Strathisla started in 1786 and also claims to be the oldest distillery in Scotland. Once called Milton distillery, its name was changed to Strathisla in the 1950s. The spring from which the distillery draws its water is reputed to have supplied water to brewers and distillers in the region for over six hundred years. Much of the whisky is used for blending, primarily in Chivas Regal.

STRATHISLA DISTILLERY

Keith
Banffshire AB55 3BS / Scotland
Tel: +44 (0)1542 783042
Visitors' center: No

REGION: Highland (Speyside)

AGE WHEN BOTTLED: 12-year-old

STRENGTH: 43%

INDEPENDENT BOTTLINGS: Blackadder, Cadenhead, Duncan Taylor & Co. (cask strength), Gordon & MacPhail

TASTING NOTES:

Aromas: Spicy, a little hot, lots of nut aromas
Flavors: Smoky, woody, nutty, long weighty finish

EST.? 1786
STRATHISLA

Strathisla Distillery KEITH · Scotland. Est? 1786

"STRATHISLA"
PURE HIGHLAND MALT
SCOTCH WHISKY
THE OLDEST DISTILLERY IN THE HIGHLANDS
AGED **12** YEARS

ML.

ALC. 43%
BY VOL.

DISTILLED AND BOTTLED BY CHIVAS BROTHERS LTD., STRATHISLA DISTILLERY, KEITH, AB55 3BS, SCOTLAND
IMPORTED BY CHIVAS BROS. IMPORT CO., NEW YORK, N.Y.
PRODUCE OF SCOTLAND

TALISKER
ISLAND (SKYE)

Talisker, the only distillery on the island of Skye, is a terrific example of the "seaweedy" character that island malts possess. One wonders if this flavor really exists or is a case of very pleasant poetic license. Appropriately, Robert Louis Stevenson in his 1880 poem "The Scottsman's Return from Abroad" called this "the king o' drinks as I conceive it, Talisker, Islay, or Glenlivit."

TALISKER DISTILLERY

Carbost
Skye IV47 8SR / Scotland
Tel: +44 (0)1478 640203 / Fax: +44 (0)1478 640401
www.malts.com
Visitors' center: Yes

REGION: Island (Skye)

AGE WHEN BOTTLED: 10-year-old, 18-year-old, 25-year-old (bottled 2001)

STRENGTH: 10-year-old: 45.8%; 18-year-old: 45.8%; 25-year-old: 57.8%

INDEPENDENT BOTTLINGS: None

TASTING NOTES:

   Aromas: Earthy, dark, smoky

   Flavors: Very peaty, woody, smoky, saline, long finish

TAMDHU
HIGHLAND (SPEYSIDE)

Very popular in England and Scotland, Tamdhu malts all of its own barley, the only distillery that does so in Speyside. The distillery was closed from 1927 until 1947. After reopening, it slowly expanded and was completely modernized in the 1980s.

TAMDHU DISTILLERY

Knockando
Aberlour
Banffshire AB38 7RP / Scotland
Tel: +44 (0)1340 870221 / Fax: +44 (0)1340 810255
Visitors' center: No

REGION: Highland (Speyside)

AGE WHEN BOTTLED: No age declaration

STRENGTH: 40%

INDEPENDENT BOTTLINGS: Adelphi, Douglas Laing, Duncan Taylor & Co. (cask strength), Gordon & MacPhail, Hart Brothers

TASTING NOTES:

   Aromas: Fruity, floral

   Flavors: Sweet, smoky, honey, and spice

TAMNAVULIN
HIGHLAND (SPEYSIDE)

In Gaelic, *tamnavulin* means "mill on the hill," which is an accurate description of this distillery that was built near an old mill, on the Glen, in the foothills of the Cairngorm Mountains in 1966. The distillery has been closed since 1996.

TAMNAVULIN DISTILLERY

Ballindaloch
Banffshire AB37 9JA / Scotland
Tel: +44 (0)1807 590 285
Visitors' center: No

REGION: Highland (Speyside)

AGE WHEN BOTTLED: 12-year-old

STRENGTH: 40.5%

INDEPENDENT BOTTLINGS: Douglas Laing, Scott's Selection

TASTING NOTES:

   Aromas: Flowery nose, light

   Flavors: Peaty, oaky, and nutty

TEANININCH

HIGHLAND

Founded in 1817 by Captain Hugh Munro, the majority of this distillery's production goes to blending. The first release of a single malt bottling was in 1992.

TEANINICH DISTILLERY

Alness
Ross-shire, IV17 0XB / Scotland
Tel: +44 (0)1349 882461 / Fax: +44 (0)1349 883864
Visitors' center: No

REGION: Highland

AGE WHEN BOTTLED: 10-year-old

STRENGTH: 43%

INDEPENDENT BOTTLINGS: Cadenhead, Chieftain's Choice, Gordon & MacPhail, Hart Brothers, SMWS

TASTING NOTES:

  Aromas: Smoky, fruity

  Flavors: Sweet, green, minty

TOBERMORY
ISLAND (MULL)

The only distillery on the island of Mull, this distillery has been closed and reopened a number of times since its founding. After being closed in 1989, the distillery was reopened in 1993. Older stocks of whisky can sometimes be found bottled under the label Ledaig. Ledaig, whose name means "safe haven" in Gaelic, is being produced again and has some pronounced peat character. Tobermorey uses unpeated malt in its production.

TOBERMORY DISTILLERY

Isle of Mull
Argyllshire PA75 6NR / Scotland
Tel: +44 (0)1688 302645 / Fax: +44 (0)1688 302643
Visitors' center: Yes

REGION: Island (Mull)

AGE WHEN BOTTLED: 10-year-old, Ledaig 15-year-old

STRENGTH: 10-year-old: 40%; Ledaig 15-year-old: 43%

INDEPENDENT BOTTLINGS: Blackadder International, Gordon & MacPhail

TASTING NOTES:

Aromas: Fresh, salty
Flavors: Sweet, minty

TOMATIN
HIGHLAND (NORTHERN)

Tomatin, one of Scotland's largest distilleries, was acquired by the Japanese in 1985 and was the first Scottish distillery to be under complete Japanese ownership. Founded in 1897 by the Tomatin Spey District Distillery Co. Ltd., this house grew from four stills in 1956 to twenty-three in 1974. Most of the malt goes for blending and export but is also available in a 12-year-old single malt bottling.

TOMATIN DISTILLERY

Tomatin
Inverness-shire IV13 7YT / Scotland
Tel: +44 (0)1808 511444 / Fax: +44 (0)1808 511373
www.tomatin.com
Visitors' center: Yes

REGION: Highland (Northern)

AGE WHEN BOTTLED: 12-year-old

STRENGTH: 40%

INDEPENDENT BOTTLINGS: Blackadder International, Cadenhead, Duncan Taylor & Co. (cask strength)

TASTING NOTES:

  Aromas: Light and sweet

  Flavors: Smoky, medium-bodied, smooth

THE FIVE BEST-SELLING WHISKIES WORLDWIDE ARE
1. GLENFIDDICH
2. GLEN GRANT
3. THE GLENLIVET
4. THE MACALLAN
5. GLENMORANGIE

TOMINTOUL
Highland (Speyside)

Two Glasgow whisky brokers established Tomintoul in 1964 in the highest village in the Scottish Highlands. It lies close to the Glenlivet area and produces a total of 1 million gallons per year. The founding brokers subsequently merged with White & Mackay, Ltd., so much of this whisky goes into White & Mackay blends.

TOMINTOUL DISTILLERY

Ballindalloch
Banffshire AB37 9AQ / Scotland
Tel: +44 (0)1807 590274 / Fax: +44 (0)1807 590342
Visitors' center: No

REGION: Highland (Speyside)

AGE WHEN BOTTLED: 10-year-old, 12-year-old, 14-year-old, 16-year-old

STRENGTH: 10-, 12-, 14, and 16-year-old: all 40%

INDEPENDENT BOTTLINGS: Adelphi, Cadenhead, Signatory

TASTING NOTES:

Aromas: Sweet, vanilla, and fruity

Flavors: Smoky and clean, slightly spicy finish

TORMORE
HIGHLAND (SPEYSIDE)

Established in 1958, this was the first distillery built in Scotland in the twentieth century. It was designed by Sir Arthur Richardson, and it is one of the most architecturally striking distilleries in Speyside.

TORMORE DISTILLERY

Grantown
North Speyside
Moray PH26 3LR / Scotland
Tel: +44 (0)1807 510244 / Fax: +44 (0)1807 510352
Visitors' center: Yes

REGION: Highland (Speyside)

AGE WHEN BOTTLED: 10-year-old, 12-year-old

STRENGTH: 10-year-old: 40%; 12-year-old: 40%

INDEPENDENT BOTTLINGS: Cadenhead, Douglas Laing

TASTING NOTES:

Aromas: Sweet spices, hint of smoke
Flavors: Caramel, fruity

TULLIBARDINE
Highland (Southern)

In 1949, Tullibardine was built on the site of a seventeenth-century brewery. The distillery was bought by Invergordon Distillers, Ltd., in 1972. The whisky production greatly benefits from the excellent water it receives from the nearby Moor of Tullibardine. Closed in 1995, Tullibardine was reopened in late 2003. A new visitors' center was constructed and informative tours of the distillery are now conducted.

TULLIBARDINE DISTILLERY

Blackford
Yachter
Perthshire PH4 1QG / Scotland
Tel: +44 (0)1764 682 252
www.tullibardine.com
Visitors' center: Yes

REGION: Highland (Southern)

AGE WHEN BOTTLED: 10-year-old

STRENGTH: 40%

INDEPENDENT BOTTLINGS: Gordon & MacPhail

TASTING NOTES:

   Aromas: Full and fruity

   Flavors: Spicy, round; peppery finish

BLENDED

CHAPTER **11** CHAPTER

WHISKIES

Variety of Flavors

Before 1853, for Scotsmen who liked their brown spirits, single malt whisky was the only drink in town, so to speak. In that year, however, the whisky merchant Andrew Usher changed everything; he's the man who is credited with inventing blended whisky.

While malt whisky is produced from 100 percent, mostly malted barley, blended whisky contains between 20 and 50 percent malt whisky. The balance is made up of grain whisky. Grain whisky differs from malt whisky in that it is made from a number of different—less expensive—grains besides barley. Also, grain whisky is produced in a continuous still, not a pot still. The upshot is that grain whisky, as compared with malt whisky, is pretty light and flavorless—not too good on its own, but just perfect for mixing with more strongly flavored whisky.

Once blended whisky was introduced, it became, for a variety of economic, social, and aesthetic reasons, synonymous with Scotch

whisky. The ease of production of this new whisky, coupled with the lighter flavor profile and consistent quality, have caught the consumer's fancy. Sales within this segment have continued a trend upward. However, over the past two decades, sales of single malt whisky have grown exponentially.

Why should this be so? Tastes definitely change. Drinkers' palates become fatigued; we become jaded in our habits. Always on the lookout for new sensations, cutting-edge consumers rediscovered the richer pleasures of single malts, the mania for consistency giving way to a spirit of adventure.

When a master blender goes about his work, adventure is definitely not on his agenda. His primary interest is to erase any and all characteristics that smack too much of regionalism, intensity, harshness, or any other quality that may be construed as too "individual." To this end, he will blend so much of this Highland whisky (for flavor) with that much Island whisky (for aroma), and that much Lowland whisky (for body). These blends may include as many as fifty single malts, which are combined in a large vat;

during the writing of this book, a new "boutique" blend was introduced that combined one hundred single malts. The master blenders all have their own recipes; one will add his predetermined percentage of grain whisky at this point, whereas another will add the grain whisky at a later stage, stir it thoroughly, and put it into the cask. One will age his whisky for a few months, but another will leave it for three to four years to "marry" the flavors. These time-honored and top-secret recipes are adhered to scrupulously, producing year in and year out the consistent blends that the consumer can taste even before they are poured into the glass.

Unlike single malt whiskies, there are no regional identifiers or any other sort of recognizable categorizations for blended whisky. As a rule of thumb, the price will indicate the quality: the more expensive the bottle, the higher the quality (and age) of the components used. As you will see in the following tasting notes, years of research and experimentation in the name of consistency have produced some really very good blended whiskies.

BLENDED WHISKY COMPARISONS
DEWAR'S

Aromas: Vaguely peppery, mild
Flavors: Slightly sweet

CHIVAS REGAL

Aromas: Wood-note, cedar
Flavors: Coffee, toffee, rich and buttery

BLACK LABEL

Aromas: Peppery, spicy
Flavors: Petrol, pepper

THE FAMOUS GROUSE

Aromas: Slightly grassy and light
Flavors: Well-balanced

THE FAMOUS GROUSE—GOLD RESERVE

Aromas: Fresh, orange peel, spices
Flavors: Orange, cinnamon, spice

THE FIVE BEST-SELLING BLENDED
WHISKIES WORLDWIDE INCLUDE
1. JOHNNIE WALKER RED LABEL
2. J & B RARE
3. BALLANTINE'S
4. GRANT'S
5. DEWAR'S

BLENDED SCOTCH WHISKY

The following is a list of the most popular blended Scotch whisky brands now available, with their age (where available) and proof.

NAME	AGE	PROOF
Ambassador	25-year-old	80 proof
Ballantine Scotch	17-year-old	86 proof
Ballantine Scotch	30-year-old	86 proof
Ballantine Scotch Finest		86 proof
Ballantine Scotch Gold Seal	12-year-old	86 proof
Barrister Scotch		80 proof
Bellows Scotch		80 proof
Black & White Scotch		80 proof
Black Bottle	10-year-old	86 proof
Black Bull Scotch		100 proof
Buchanan's Scotch	12-year-old	80 proof
Buchanan's Scotch Deluxe	18-year-old	80 proof
Bullock & Lade (B & L) Scotch		80 proof
Chivas Regal Royal Salute	21-year-old	80 proof
Chivas Regal Scotch	12-year-old	80 proof
Clan MacGregor Scotch		80 proof
Claymore Scotch		80 proof
Cluny Scotch	12-year-old	80 proof
Compass Box "Asyla"	12-year-old	80 proof
Crawford's Scotch		80 proof
Crown Sterling Scotch		80 proof
Cutty Sark Scotch		80 proof
Desmond & Duff Scotch	12-year-old	80 proof
Dawson		80 proof
Dew of Ben Nevis		86 proof

Dewar's Signature		80 proof
Dewar's White Label	12-year-old	80 proof
Glenalmond Scotch	10-year-old	80 proof
Glenandrew Scotch	10-year-old	
Glenandrew Scotch	15-year-old	
Glenandrew Scotch	20-year-old	
Grand Macnich Scotch		80 proof
Grand Old Parr Scotch Deluxe	12-year-old	86 proof
Grant's		80 proof
Grant's Scotch Blended	25-year-old	86 proof
Grant's Scotch Heritage		80 proof
Hankey Bannister Scotch		86 proof
Hartley Parker's Scotch		80 proof
Harvey's Scotch		80 proof
Heather Glen Scotch		80 proof
House of Stuart Scotch	4-year-old	80 proof
Inver House Scotch Rare Inverarity Scotch Blended		80 proof
J & B Scotch J.E.T.	15-year-old	86 proof
J & B Scotch Rare		80 proof
J & B Scotch Select		80 proof
J & B Ultima		86 proof
J. W. Dant Scotch		80 proof
John Barr Scotch Gold Label		80 proof
John Barr Scotch Special Reserve Black Label		86 proof
John Begg Scotch Blue Cap		86 proof
John Player Scotch		80 proof

CONTINUED >

NAME	AGE	PROOF
Johnnie Walker Scotch Black Label	12-year-old	86.8 proof
Johnnie Walker Scotch Blue Label		80 proof
Johnnie Walker Scotch Gold Label	18-year-old	80 proof
Johnnie Walker Scotch Green Label	15-year-old	80 proof
Johnnie Walker Scotch Red Label		80 proof
Jon, Mark & Robbo "The Smoky, Peaty One"		80 proof
King George IV Scotch		80 proof
King William IV Scotch		80 proof
Lauder's Scotch		80 proof
Legacy Scotch		80 proof
McColl's Scotch		80 proof
McGregor Scotch Perfection		80 proof
Michel Courveur "Unfiltered" Scotch	12-year-old	80 proof
Old Smuggler Scotch		80 proof
Passport Scotch		80 proof

Peter Dawson Scotch Special		80 proof
Pig's Nose	5-year-old	80 proof
Pinch "Dimple" Scotch	15-year-old	86 proof
Piper 100 Scotch		80 proof
Poland Spring Scotch		80 proof
Queen Anne Scotch		80 proof
Royal Salute Scotch		80 proof
Scoresby Scotch Very Rare		80 proof
Sheep Dip	21-year-old	80 proof
Tambowie Scotch		80 proof
Teacher's Scotch Highland Cream		86 proof
The Famous Grouse Scotch	12-year-old	80 proof
The Famous Grouse Scotch Gold Reserve		80 proof
The Famous Grouse Vintage Malt	1992 Vintage	80 proof
Usher's Scotch Green Stripe		82 proof
Vat 69		80 proof
White Horse Scotch		80 proof
Whiteside Scotch Blended		86.8 proof

A SINGLE MALT SCOTCH MENU

With the increasing popularity of single malts, many fine restaurants have added a separate Scotch listing to their wine and after-dinner drink lists. Keens Steakhouse, a venerable institution in New York City, has one of the best on-premises single malt lists that we have seen:

Keens STEAKHOUSE

SINGLE MALT SCOTCHES

SCOTCH	YEARS AGED	PRICE
HIGHLAND MALTS		
ARDBEG	20	12.00
BALBLAIR	10	9.50
CLYNELISH	22	20.00
DALLAS DHU	1974	15.50
DALMORE	12	8.00
DALMORE STILLMANS DRAM	26	15.00
DALWHINNIE	15	9.50
EDRADOUR	10	9.00
GLEN EDEN	NV	6.75
GLENGOYNE	10	9.00
GLENGOYNE	17	12.50
GLENGOYNE	1967	24.00
GLENKEITH	1983	9.00
GLENLOCHY	25	23.00
GLENMORANGIE	10	7.50
GLENMORANGIE	18	10.50
GLENMORANGIE	12 *PORT*	15.00
GLENMORANGIE	12 *SHERRY*	10.00
GLENMORANGIE	12 *MADEIRA*	10.00
GLENMORANGIE	1971	26.50
GLEN ROTHES	1974	14.00
GLEN ROTHES	1979	11.00
INCHMURRIN	10	7.50
LOCH DHU BLACK	10	8.00
OBAN	14	9.00
OLD FETTERCAIRN	10	6.75
ROYAL LOCHNAGAR	12	9.00
ROYAL LOCHNAGAR	RESERVE	25.00
TOMINTOUL	1971	13.00
TULLIBARDINE	10	5.50
HIGHLAND/SPEYSIDE		
ABERFELDY	1978	11.00
ABERLOUR	10	8.00
ABERLOUR	1970	19.50
BALVENIE	10	9.50
BALVENIE	12	9.00
BALVENI	15	10.00
BENRIACH	10	9.00
BENRIACH	1982	15.50
CARDHU	12	8.50
CRAGGANMORE	12	9.00
DUFTOWN	13	17.00
GLENDRONACH	12	9.50
GLENDRONACH	15	10.00
GLENDEVERON	12	6.75
GLENFARCLAS	10	7.00
GLENFARCLAS	12	7.50
GLENFARCLAS	25	15.50
GLENFIDDICH	12	7.00
GLENFIDDICH	18	18.00
GLENFORRES	12	5.50
GLENLIVET	12	7.00
GLENLIVET	18	11.00
GLENTROMIE	12	8.00

SCOTCH	YEARS AGED	PRICE
HIGHLAND/SPEYSIDE—Cont.		
LINKWOOD	21	13.50
LONGMORN	1981	10.50
GLEN GARIOCH	8	6.75
GLEN GARIOCH	12	7.00
GLEN GARIOCH	15	8.50
GLEN GARIOCH	21	13.00
GLEN GLASSAUGH	12	6.75
GLEN MORAY	12	8.00
GLEN ORD	12	9.00
INCHGOWER	1980	10.50
KNOCKANDO	1980	10.00
KNOCKANDO	18	12.50
KNOCKANDO	25	25.00
KNOCKANDO	1970	27.00
MACALLAN	12	9.00
MACALLAN	18	12.00
MACALLAN	25	25.00
MORTLACH	22	19.50
STRATHISALA	12	9.00
TAMDHU	10	7.50
TORMORE	5	6.25
LOWLAND		
AUCHENTOSHAN	NV	7.00
AUCHENTOSHAN	10	9.50
AUCHENTOSHAN	21	16.50
GLENKINCHE	10	9.00
INVERARITY	10	9.00
LITTLE MILL	8	7.50
PRIME MALT #1	15	8.50
ROSEBANK	1974	11.50
ISLAY		
BRUICHLADDICH	10	8.50
BRUICHLADDICH	15	10.50
BRUICHLADDICH	21	15.50
BOWMORE LEGEND	NV	7.50
BOWMORE	10	8.50
BOWMORE	17	10.50
BOWMORE	21	16.50
BOWMORE BLACK	25	18.50
BUNNAHABHAIN	1964	56.00
LAPHROAIG	12	9.50
LAPHROAIG	10	9.00
LAGAVULIN	15	13.00
PORT ELLEN	16	10.00
	16	11.50
CAMPLETOWN		
DRAM SELECT	23	16.50
DRAM SELECT	21	14.50
GLEN SCOTIA	12	8.50
SPRINGBANK	12	10.50
SPRINGBANK 100p	12	11.00
SPRINGBANK	15	12.50
SPRINGBANK	1979	13.00
SPRINGBANK	21	15.00
SPRINGBANK	25	22.00
ISLE OF MULL		
TOBERMORY	NV	7.00
DRAM SELECT	21	14.50
OLD MELDRUM		
MICHEL COUVIER	15	10.50
ISLAND MALTS		
HIGHLAND PARK	12	8.50
SCAPA	1979	10.50
SCAPA	12	9.00
TALISKER	10	9.50
IRISH SINGLE MALT		
BUSHMILLS	10	8.00
BUSHMILLS	16	11.50
* MIDLETON VERY RARE	BLEND	16.50

ALL SCOTCHES SUBJECT TO AVAILABILITY

GLOSSARY

BLENDED WHISKY
A combination of grain and malt whiskies, popular for their lighter styles of flavor.

CASK
A wooden barrel used to age Scotch whisky.

CONTINUOUS STILL
A coffey still, as opposed to a pot still, consists of two columns that do not need to be refilled, but can be used continuously. This process is used for making a lighter Scotch whisky typically used for blends.

DIASTASE
An enzyme contained within grain that allows starch to become soluble. The next step in distillation is to turn that starch into sugar.

DRAFF
The remaining grain, generally barley, left in the mash tun after the wort is drawn off. This material is dried and used as cattle feed.

FEINTS
The distillate that remains after the middle cut, or best bottling whisky, has been drawn off. Feints contain high levels of alcohol and impurities and are typically blended with the foreshots and the wash and redistilled.

FINISHING
A form of aging. Certain whisky will be put into various types of casks to marry and age.

FORESHOTS
The first part of the distillate to come out of the second kettle of the pot still. The foreshots have low alcohol levels and impurities and are therefore not bottled. They are saved and redistilled with the feints.

GRAIN WHISKY
Whisky made in a patent still. The primary grain is usually corn.

INDEPENDENT BOTTLER
A broker or firm that will seek out or contract with malt distilleries to purchase individual casks of malt whisky. The independent bottler uses its own private label usually indicating the origin of the distillery on it. Examples of classic independent bottlers are Cadenhead, Gordons & MacPhail, and the Scotch Malt Whisky Society.

LOW WINES
The distillate produced in the first kettle of the pot still. It contains alcohol, other chemical compounds of both pure and impure natures, and a bit of water. The low wines are redistilled in the spirit still.

MALT
Any grain whose starch has been converted into sugar; the primary sugar is maltose.

MASHING
Mixing dried ground malt with hot water.

MIDDLE CUT
The best of the distillate from the spirit still, as determined by the still operator. This is the only portion of the distillate that is bottled.

PATENT STILL
Also called the continuous still, it can operate without interruption, unlike the pot still that needs to be cleaned and recharged after each pass. The production from the continuous still is a clean, light, rather characterless spirit, generally used for the production of grain alcohol.

PEAT
There are two kinds of peat: marsh and forest. Marsh peat is made up of decomposed mosses. Forest peat is made up of decomposed branches and leaves. When used as a fuel source for drying malted barley, the peat imparts a distinctive flavor to malt whisky.

POT STILL
A pair of copper kettles with coils at the top, heated by coal or steam. In the first of the two, called the wash still, the fermented liquid is heated to the boiling point and vaporizes into the coils. The coils are cooled and the vapor is condensed and collected. The production from the first still, known as the low wines, is put through the second vessel, called the spirit still, and malt whisky emerges.

PROOF
The alcoholic strength of the spirit, measured with a hydrometer.

RECTIFY
To dilute with a percentage of water to achieve a uniform proof.

SACCHARIFY
The production of sugar during the malting and soaking process. The enzyme diastase is released inside the barley during this process. The starch inside the grain is turned into sugar, hence, to saccharify.

SINGLE MALT WHISKY
The production of an individual distillery.

SPIRIT STILL
The second of the two pot stills producing the high concentration finished alcohol spirit that will be directly placed in casks. (See *wash still.*)

UISGE BEATHA
Gaelic for "water of life." Over the centuries, this term was shortened, anglicized, and ultimately rendered as *whisky.*

WASH
The fermented wort. This liquid is placed in the pot still for the first distillation.

WASH STILL
The first of the two pot stills typical to Scotch whisky that will produce low-concentration low wines.

WORT
The liquid that is produced by soaking malted barley in warm water in a large tub called a mash tun. This liquid contains sugars and other components that, with the addition of brewer's yeast, transform it into alcohol.

RESOURCE GUIDE

BOOKS

Jackson, Michael. *Complete Guide to Single Malt Scotch*. 5th ed. Philadelphia: Running Press Publishers, 2004.

___. *Whisky: The Definitive Guide*. New York: DK Publishers, 2005.

___. *Malt Whisky*. London: Mitchell Beazley Publishers, 2002.

MacLean, Charles. *Scotch Whisky: A Liquid History*. London: Cassell Publishers, 2003.

Murray, Jim. *Jim Murray's Whisky Bible 2005*. London: Carlton Publishing Group, 2004.

MAGAZINES

THE MALT ADVOCATE
www.maltadvocate.com
This magazine highlights current news items and gives good brand analysis.

WHISKY MAGAZINE
www.whiskymag.com
This is a helpful guide, including tasting notes on numerous brands.

WEB SITES

MALT MADNESS
www.maltmadness.com
This is a highly opinionated Web site with idiosyncratic reviews of many, many malts.

PEAT FREAK
www.peatfreak.com
Use this site for helpful information on planning distillery visits.

SCOTCH WHISKY ASSOCIATION
www.Scotch-whisky.org
This is a good source for maps of the whisky regions of Scotland.

SCOTCHWHISKY.NET
www.scotchwhisky.net
This popular Web site gives a very thorough overview of the world of whisky and has helpful links to independent bottlers.

SCOTLAND'S MALT WHISKY TRAIL
www.Maltwhiskytrail.com
At this Web site, you will find more helpful information for those contemplating a whisky tour of Scotland.

RETAIL SOURCES, USA:
PARK AVENUE LIQUORS
292 Madison Avenue
New York, NY 10017
www.parkaveliquor.com

SAM'S WINES AND SPIRITS
1720 North Marcy Street
Chicago, IL 60614
www.samswine.com

THE WHISKY SHOP
76 Geary Street
San Francisco, CA 94108
www.scotchwhisky.net

RETAIL SOURCES, UK
LOCH FYNE WHISKIES
Inveraray
Argyll PH 32 8UD
Scotland
Tel: +44(0)11499 302 219
www.lfw.co.uk

MILROY'S OF SOHO
3 Greek Street
London W1D 4NA
United Kingdom
Tel: +44 (0)274372385
www.milroys.co.uk

INDEX

ILLUSTRATIONS ARE INDICATED IN **BOLD**.

PHOTO CREDITS

T=TOP; M= MIDDLE; B=BOTTOM; L=LEFT; R=RIGHT